Dogsled Apostles

† Joseph R. Crimont, S.J.

Dogsled Apostles

by

A. H. Savage

NEW YORK · 1942

Sheed & Ward

TO

MY MOTHER AND FATHER

IN LOVING MEMORY

Preface

FOR ALMOST FIFTY YEARS the Most Reverend Joseph Raphael Crimont, S.J. has presided over his scattered flock in Alaska. During 1942 he commemorated the twenty-fifth anniversary of his episcopal consecration and continued, at 84, as the oldest bishop in point of years in the American hierarchy.

There have been scattered accounts of this veteran apostle and his trailmakers in the far north, but there has never before been a composite picture of their stirring lives. In DOGSLED APOSTLES we see the missionaries at work amongst the natives, sowing the seed of the gospel, not by word of mouth alone, but by the labor and toil of their hands, sharing with their people their food, their every privation. Real heroes pass before our eyes. There is, for instance Father Monroe whose exploits will stir the blood of even the coldest heart, and Father Lucchesi whose heroic work in the epidemic on the Yukon lifts one up.

We need literature in a form and style that will reach beyond our mission minded public. I believe that DOGSLED APOSTLES achieves a new note in this field. It is so filled with human interest that the attention of the reader never wavers. I am proud to claim a remote part in its publication. After hearing the author describe her first Alaskan trip, I encouraged her to return with the idea of writing this book.

The story has everything we want: truth well recorded, style vivid and graphic in its simplicity, wit and humor, and a genuine appreciation of the sublime vocation of a Catholic missionary. The spirit of Bishop Crimont permeates the pages as the labors of his early confreres are unfolded. After reading DOGSLED APOSTLES we can never forget the exploits of these Apostles of the north, for their Christlike characters sound the depths of our better selves. We who are endeavoring to spread the mission spirit are indebted to the author for her splendid support.

MOST REVEREND RICHARD J. CUSHING, D.D.
Boston Diocesan Director of the Society
for the Propagation of the Faith.

Acknowledgments

M Y GRATITUDE EXTENDS beyond the space for acknowledgments. Those who have given me the greatest help are:

Bishop Walter J. Fitzgerald, Very Rev. Joseph F. McElmeel, Rev. Patrick O'Reilly, Rev. John P. Fox, Rev. Paul C. O'Connor, Rev. Francis M. Menager, Rev. James Spils, Rev. Wm. G. LeVasseur, Rev. J. I. McHugh, all of the Society of Jesus; Rev. James Snead; Sister M. Eulalia, Sister M. Angela, Sister M. Magdalen of the Sacred Heart, all of them members of the Congregation of Sisters of St. Ann; and Sister M. Theodula, S.P., all still in Alaska.

Bishop Richard J. Cushing, Rev. Artheme Dutilly, O.M.I., Rev. John J. Wynne, S.J., Rev. Ambrose Gallagher, Rev. Bernard Hubbard, S.J., Rev. Calvert Alexander, S.J., Rev. Harold Gardiner, S.J., Rev. John Cantillon, S.J., Sister M. Perpetual Help, S.S.A. (R.I.P.), Sister M. Gabriella, S.S.A., Sister M. Bertrande, D.C., Sister M. Calasanctius, S.S.A.

Mr. and Mrs. Thomas Riggs, Mr. Edwin Edgerly, Mr. Gregory Landon, S.J., Mr. Maurice L. Sharp, Mr. Otto William Geist, Mr. J. O'Connor, Miss Bertha Tiber, Miss Patricia Edgerly, Miss Frances Ross, and Miss Adelaide Jones.

My specially grateful acknowledgment goes to Rev. Basil Matthews, O.S.B., for his criticism and editorial assistance.

Contents

Bibliography

Published Works:

BARNUM, F., S.J.: U. S. Catholic Historical Society, Vol. XIII, May, 1919.

CALASANCTIUS, M.: *Voice of Alaska,* Srs. of St. Ann Press, Lachine, Quebec, 1935.

CANADA'S WESTERN NORTHLAND, Ottawa, 1937.

CATHOLIC DIRECTORIES, annual, since 1875, Kenedy, N. Y.

DENTAL CARIES, American Dental Association, N. Y., 1940.

DEPARTMENT OF COMMERCE, *Bureau of Fisheries Bulletins,* Washington, D. C.

DUCHAUSSOIS, P., O.M.I.: *Mid Ice and Snow,* Kenedy, N. Y., 1923.

JENNESS, D.: *Indians of Canada,* National Museum, Ottawa, 1930.

JESUIT MISSION MAGAZINES, files of, New York.

MIRSKY, J.: *To the North,* Viking, N. Y., 1934.

NORTHWEST TERRITORIES, Ottawa, 1930.

THEODORA, M.: *Heralds of Christ the King,* Kenedy, N. Y., 1939.

WOODSTOCK LETTERS, files of, Woodstock, Md.

Unpublished Works:

JETTE, J., S.J.: *The Jottings of an Alaskan Missionary.*

LaFORTUNE, B., S.J.: Diary of.

MONROE, F., S.J.: *Beginnings at Eagle.*

PERRON, J., S.J.: *Origins of Holy Cross.*

Missionary Priests and their Location in Alaska in the fall of 1942

(All except the nine starred belong to the Society of Jesus)

Most Rev. Joseph R. Crimont, Bishop, Juneau

Most Rev. Walter J. Fitzgerald, Co-adjutor Bishop, Fairbanks

Very Rev. Joseph F. McElmeel, Superior General, Nulato and Fairbanks

Indian and Eskimo Villages

Rev. Edmund A. Anable, Holy Cross
Rev. John B. Baud, Nulato
Rev. Jules Convert, Hooper Bay
Rev. Thomas J. Cunningham, Diomede Island
Rev. Paul C. Deschout, Nelson Island
Rev. George Endal, Mountain Village
Rev. John P. Fox, Hooper Bay
Rev. Bellarmine Lafortune, King Island
Rev. Segundo Llorente, Akulurak
Rev. Martin Lonneux, St. Michael
Rev. Francis M. Menager, Bethel
Rev. Paul C. O'Connor, Kotzebue
Rev. James Spils, Holy Cross

Parishes in Towns

*Rev. Harley Baker, Skagway
Rev. Edward Budde, Juneau
*Rev. William Chaput, Seward
*Rev. Leo A. Dufour, Army Chaplain
Rev. Aloysius S. Eline, Fairbanks

xiv

REV. WM. G. ELLIOTT, FAIRBANKS
*REV. G. EDGAR GALLANT, SKAGWAY
*REV. MATTHEW A. HOCH, WRANGELL
REV. WILLIAM G. LE VASSEUR, JUNEAU
REV. NATALIS J. MARUCA, KETCHIKAN
REV. JOSEPH I. MCHUGH, NOME
*REV. DERMOT O'FLANAGAN, ANCHORAGE
REV. PATRICK J. O'REILLY, SITKA
*REV. TIMOTHY O'RYAN, ABSENT ON LEAVE
*REV. JAMES P. SNEAD, ANCHORAGE
*REV. MERRILL SULZMAN, AUXILIARY CHAPLAIN,
ANNETTE ISLAND

I

Voyage to Alaska

[1894]

*I*T ALL *began quite innocently as a vacation trip to Alaska, and a proposed interview with the oldest Bishop of America. But the visit mysteriously took on larger proportions, and almost before I knew it, I was devoting most of my waking moments to an interview which wanted to grow into a book. On returning to the States I found myself telling people of Bishop Crimont, and—whether in Seattle, San Francisco, St. Paul, New York or Boston—others were always as eager to talk of him as I was. A word-of-mouth Crimontana was growing up over the country.*

I returned to Juneau the following May, and spent all of that summer in Alaska. Each morning exactly at ten Bishop Crimont would come over from the hospital, put his hat on the rack in the hall, and we would begin working in the parlor of the rectory. The first day he began, not with his own life, but with that of Father Francis Monroe whose friendship he had shared from 1873 to 1940, and whose tremendous heroism had only come to light two years before. These memories quite naturally carried him into his own life, and as he dipped back into the memories of his childhood and youth, I took notes.

"See," he would say when we covered some seeming unproductive ground, "you will be sorry that you ever undertook this." Then would follow some fascinating material that would bring me to the edge of my chair in my eagerness not to miss a word.

Soon the rustiness of remembering was gone, and after a few days the Bishop was talking for as much as an hour and a half without stopping. He said he thought it was a disadvantage for a lad to have an excellent memory: in his formative years

2

he himself had memorized his lessons without effort, and this facility prevented him from developing his memory, consequently, later he did not have a good one.

But he had no trouble recalling people's entire names, with their exact spelling, no matter how long before he had known them. After a few days he said, "You might really get my memory to come back again." Then it was I suspected that his memory was actually one in a thousand. It came about in this way. I asked how young he was when he had thought of becoming a priest, and he said quite definitely: "Why I told you that last summer." In looking back in my notes of the preceding August, I found the place. His keenness continued to be a source of joy. And his generous appreciation was good to have.

Meanwhile I made out lists of questions which he said he would put at the feet of St. Terese so that she would inspire him with the answers. Every day his correspondence piled higher, and on some days he would let me help him with it. A new and fresh sense of the magic of words came to me as he dictated the answers. His expression was exquisitely clear, cameo-like, with a French economy of words, a preciseness in their choice, and a here-and-nowness that focused what he said. And with it all there was never any rush to finish a given amount. Painstaking care was given each letter, with never a suggestion of a deadline. Usually he writes all his letters by hand, for he has no secretary, nor has he ever had one.

During this time he was having electrical treatments for his chest where he had bumped into a chair. Though it pained him when he coughed, the nurse did not suggest that he go to bed because of the danger of bad circulation in one his age.

He said that a missionary ought to be not a man but an angel, a pure spirit without any material needs, since it was so difficult to get enough money to live on. Perhaps not alone financial worries, but the condition of his feet made him think of this solution. My first knowledge of these bunions came one day when he mentioned that his feet were so bad he sometimes thought he would like to walk on his knees.

Through the weeks the Bishop told me the stories of his contemporaries—Father Monroe, Father Lucchesi, Father Jette, Father Judge—and loaned me all the available material about the early days on the missions. He was more ready to tell me stories of them than of himself. And here it was I first learned that the extreme modesty of the missionaries which made the gathering of material sometimes difficult, had, beyond the spirit of humility, an actual basis in circumstance. For as one of them later told me:

"In New York you may be interested in reading of a man getting lost for several days in a blizzard, having to dig into the snow until it blows over, and meanwhile running out of food. We all have such experiences—not only the missionaries, but the other townspeople, the prospectors, the trappers. So there is no point in telling these stories as examples of hardships. They are in the order of the day."

Meanwhile the early summer was beautiful in Juneau. Though it rained almost every morning, the afternoon usually cleared so that you could see across the Gastineau channel to Douglas Island with its snow-covered mountains. Juneau is actually carved out of the side of the mountain, and the streets are terraced ribbons against the green.

The next two months found me in the interior of Alaska, the stage on which these heroic figures played their parts.

THE YOUNG PRIEST had crossed the Atlantic five times before in the past eight years. Then he had been ill for short periods only. But this small freighter, the sport of the billows of the Pacific, was trial enough even to the stoutest sailor.

It was July of the year of Our Lord 1894. Dark cabins served as staterooms, the deck space was crammed with bags of coal. Getting fresh air, even on sunny days was a real problem. The merest whiff was a great luxury. Trying to walk meant falling and rolling over coal sacks; sitting on them was an invitation to the salty spray. Time and again the interminable stretches of rough sea threatened to wash cargo, passengers, crew and boat into the bosom of the ocean. The voyage was one prolonged nightmare.

The boat's excessive cargo made it a challenge to the angry waves. But it was a profitable if not comfortable way of getting from Seattle to Alaska. It belonged to the North Transportation and Trading Company who were bringing coal, lumber and food supplies to their store at Forty Mile on the upper Yukon. The passengers, however, were being carried more by the way of accommodation than as a source of revenue, and the crew had given up its quarters to them with more grace than might have been expected. But by the time the boat had found its way down Elliot Bay, through the green-fringed straits to the sea, the passengers had already discovered that these berths were cages for cramped and aching bones.

Joseph Raphael Crimont, ordained just six years before was now, in 1894, in his thirty-seventh year. Already some 6000 miles from Ferrieres, France, where he was born, he was on his first trip to Alaska. Mr. and Mrs. Patrick Galvin came from Helena, Montana and were on their way to Forty Mile River where, as tin-smith, Mr. Galvin had previously spent a year. The remaining passengers consisted of six utterly unhappy Eskimo, and the two white men who had exhibited them at the Chicago Fair. Living always at Port Clarence on Seward Peninsula north of Nome, the Eskimo had been accustomed to bitter cold winters and cool summers. The heat of Chicago's sun had been too much for them, especially for their chief who seemed to feel too dejected to care whether he ever reached home: he looked silently across the blue waters to the north, his eyes glazed and hopeless. From the bottom of the hold to the level of the deck a place had been walled up with planks to receive the Eskimo, separating them from the bulk of the inner cargo. No wonder they fared badly.

Several times during that part of the trip from Seattle to Unalaska the Scandinavian Captain visited the berth of the young missionary priest who had eaten nothing since Victoria. He was severely stricken with sea-sickness. Under his pillow lay a bottle of brandy, but only on the first day did he taste that. The rest he presented to the Captain who made no delay in cheering himself with the potion. These circumstances were not distressing enough; one thing more happened to add to this sadly memorable trip.

While the Captain was visiting one who he thought was a dying man, the Eskimo chief, at the bottom of the suffocating shaft was actually at death's door. He had tried valiantly to hold out until he reached home, but before the Aleutian Islands came into sight, death had claimed him.

Since land was near, they decided not to bury him at sea, but to keep the body wrapped in canvas until they reached Unalaska. Meanwhile, a heavy fog surrounded the boat so that they could see nothing but grey mist closing in on them. At this stage the Captain cast anchor. A few minutes later the echo of the whistle blasts told them that they were locked in by land or rocks. The schooner settled down to await more favorable weather and the sailors, freed from care, immediately began to fish, catching great quantities of fresh morue, or Canadian black cod. When late in the afternoon of that day, the fog cleared, the Captain was amazed to find that the boat was entirely rockbound, and that just ahead of the prow the jagged points lay half submerged in the dark waters. With painstaking industry he maneuvered the boat free of the rocks and guided it safely along the big sand-pit leading to Unalaska.

Father Crimont knew on reaching the harbor that there was work to be done. As soon as the boat stopped rolling, his nausea ceased, and he quickly got well. First, he obtained permission from the Russian deacon to bury the Eskimo chief in the town cemetery. When it was ready, two white men brought and lowered the corpse into the freshly dug grave, while Father Crimont performed the last rites. The funeral over, he returned to the deacon's residence to bring back the tools and to drink a glass of Russian tea, the first he had ever tasted.

The boat remained a few days at Dutch Harbor. From this time on the young priest got sick no more. They were actually only 750 miles from St. Michael now, but the Alaskan waters were strange to the Captain. Instead of going directly, he sailed northeast from the Aleutian Islands and arrived within sight of Cape Nome before he realized he was too far north. Here he turned, making a right-angle across Norton Sound.

It would seem a simple thing for a boat merely to find the mouth of the Yukon and sail up the river to Holy Cross and beyond it, to Forty Mile. But the mouth of the Yukon is so complex and treacherous that in order to get to the river's main course a seaman must have a thorough knowledge of the peculiarities of the delta. The Russians learned when they first began trading in this region that the ocean was shallow far out from the delta and that the river had built up at the mouth hundreds of miles of silt through which run many branches and sloughs (rhyme with blues).

Because of this, the port for the unloading of ocean freight had to be established, not at the mouth, but 75 miles north of it. Thus, in the early days, St. Michael came into being.

The arrival of the boat, of course, caused great excitement in the town, especially amongst a group of Eskimo boys surrounding two men dressed in black. One of these men, no longer able to contain his curiosity, borrowed a canoe from an Eskimo and paddled out to meet the boat.

That August day was a heavy, humid one, and it was only by the sound of bells that the shore and the newly arrived boat could signal to each other. Consequently, the crew, Mr. and Mrs. Galvin, the two other white men, what was left of the Eskimos, and the young missionary, heard the bells as chimes from an unseen world. Impatiently they waited. They waited while the first lighter came out to get the freight, and they waited, baggage packed and ready, until the time came for them to climb down the ladder to the barge. The deck was cleared of some of the bags of coal at the first transshipment, which allowed Father Crimont to indulge in the luxury of a few unhampered strides in the clearance. He was impatient to see this new land and now after two thousand miles of rough ocean, it was still hidden in the fog.

He was strolling along the deck when suddenly a familiar voice reached his ear. Although he did not immediately recognize the owner, he felt like shouting for joy and he darted toward the prow where Mr. Hamilton was supervising the unloading.

"Where are the missionaries?" the voice was demanding. "Where are they?"

Before Mr. Hamilton had a chance to answer, Father Crimont arrived and smiled down at the interrogator with the familiar voice.

"Here they are all wrapped in one," he called.

The occupant of the boat looked stunned. "Is it you, poor little Crim? Oh my, we don't want you. You aren't made for this kind of country. In a few weeks you'll be dead. Stay on the boat and go back. It's the only way to do."

Joseph Raphael Crimont and Francis Barnum had been classmates at Woodstock in Maryland, and while the former had been ordained in 1888 and had then been sent to work among the Crow Indians, Francis Barnum had been one of the first American fathers to volunteer for the Alaskan mission. It was he and Father Robaut who had impatiently awaited the long overdue boat. They not only expected the annual supplies of food for their missions, but they had hoped against hope for the arrival of at least several Jesuit Fathers and some Sisters.

At this time there were only nine Jesuits in Alaska and six Sisters of Saint Ann. Holy Cross on the Yukon River was their first mission and working out from it a few stations had been established. Here in 1888 Father Robaut with a few Brothers and three Sisters of St. Ann had begun the boarding school for native children. Now six years later there were resident priests at Nulato, at Nukluroyit, and on Nelson Island. Besides these missions for the natives, Father Judge was soon to begin his heroic career at Forty Mile camp near which he was but a few years later to give up his life nursing the miners.

The Eskimo villages on Kotzebue Sound north of

Nome, and those on the Kuskokwim River south of the Yukon, had great need of missionaries, but there were not enough of them to go around, and the work had to wait.

When Father Crimont reached the shore with his carpet bag the best he could do, he said, was to kiss the ground, to thank God for his land of adoption. It was his first meeting with Aloysius Robaut whose advice was much like that of Father Barnum.

"You have no idea what these winters are like," he said.

"You've managed them, though," the new arrival remarked.

It is true that no one would have picked this slight man for a missionary in the far north. His life, with the exception of two years with the Crow Indians, had been that of a scholar. He had fine features, rather on the pale side, with dark hair and serene blue eyes. Early in his Jesuit novitiate he had aspired to become a missionary, but during his frail youth and student days it was considered impossible by his superiors. How he became stronger is part of this story. Suffice now to say that he had arrived in this mission field which, though seemingly demanding a rugged, robust constitution would yet treat with kindness this little man whose spirit and zeal outstripped the vigor of his physique.

When the fog lifted later in the day, the young missionary enjoyed his first blue Alaskan skies with their huge billowy clouds. He sniffed in vain for the spruce-scented air, for St. Michael, the gateway to Alaska's vast interior, was filled with tundra, plentiful with flowers, ferns, yellowish brown grass, luxurious with game, but it had no trees. The land especially here along the coast, was bleak, and except for a handful of white men in the government service or those running the trading post, the country appeared suitable only for Eskimo.

He watched the natives' great skill in maneuvering their light sealskin boats. On shore they stood about with shy, infrequent smiles, waiting to trade their furs and ivory craftmanship for foodstuffs for the year. They seemed more at home in a boat. As was customary they combined trading expeditions with boat excursions in which their whole family took part. The children hid behind their mothers' skirts, and the sleeping brown babies nestled in gay-colored shawls against their mothers' backs.

For the young priest who was later to become the first Bishop of Alaska, and who despite his frail health, would outlive all the rest, this was an unforgettable day. The two missionaries gave him first-hand knowledge of the work: Father Robaut who had accompanied Archbishop Seghers on his martyr journey along the Yukon, and Father Barnum who for three years had worked at the mission on Bering Sea. Both told him the story of their work; and both, as was characteristic of missionaries, told what had happened without bringing into the picture themselves, their reactions, or their sufferings. For their fellow workers they had nothing but praise; for themselves, understatement.

With the experience of his ordeal at sea behind him the new apostle felt his health come back to him again with a rebound. His nature rejoiced within him and the gay blue skies and the cheerfulness of his confreres synchronized to make the joy of his first day full. He breathed deeply of the sea air. It smelled very good.

St. Michael, gateway to the interior.

Archbishop Seghers.

Bishop Crimont.

Father LaFortune.

Father Lucchesi.

II

The Russian Empire in Alaska

[1799-1867]

A TRAVELER in Alaska soon senses in the ground beneath him the roots of the race that is there no more. The Aleutian Islands especially are full of Russian names—Mount Veniaminof, Shelikof Strait, Shumagin Islands. The Russian Cathedral in Sitka (first called New Archangel) still contains elegant vestments embroidered with pure gold thread, a crucifix inlaid in pearl, an icon representing the Annunciation carved in ivory, and the famous Sitka Madonna.

Each morning and afternoon on my way to the Bishop's house, I passed the home of the late Rev. A. P. Kashevaroff, who until he died was the famous curator of the Museum in Juneau. One dismal rainy morning I watched workmen tear down the house.

THE TERRITORY OF ALASKA had become a part of the United States only twenty-seven years before the arrival of Joseph Raphael Crimont in 1894. In these early years the Russian influence was still visible on every side—the language, the buildings, the faces of its people bore witness to it. *The Jottings of an Alaskan Missionary* written by Father Julius Jette throw an illuminating light on the progress of this period. Let him guide us on our tour of early missions.

One hundred and sixty-six years before our story begins, Vitus Bering, a Dane in the service of the Russian navy, first sailed along the Siberian Coast and through Bering Strait. He had no idea, as he peered through the fog, that the American mainland was only sixty miles east of his course. Ten years later, in 1738, the Russian Empress, Ann, sent him on the second expedition, and this time he sailed to Kamtchatka, establishing in 1740 the settlement of Petropaulovsk. The next year he passed down through the Aleutian Islands and reached the southern coast of the Alaska Peninsula, following it to Cape St. Elias. A member of his crew, Shumagin by name, was buried on one of the Islands and hence the naming of the whole group of fifteen islands after him. The same year the explorer's ship was wrecked on Bering Island where he died in December. The survivors of the expedition wintered there, and after many hardships finally reached home, where they confirmed the existence of the long-disputed Aleutian Islands as well as of a neighboring mainland.

Thus Alaska was discovered, its name being the English version of the native term, Al-ay-ek-sa meaning The Great Land.

The traders, trappers and fur hunters lost no time in getting acquainted with the Aleutians. Their exploitation began the same year that Bering's men returned, and history tells us they searched, sacked and combed the Islands with varying degrees of unscrupulousness. Glottof, a trader, made a map showing eight islands in the Aleutian string east of Unalaska, and in that year, 1759, baptized the son of a native chief. A huge cross was erected on his Island to commemorate the event. It was evidently not so much the love of God, but rather business considerations that prompted these first baptisms, for converted natives not only became more manageable but were more willing to give their trade exclusively to their godfathers.

In 1760 another trader named Andreian Tolstykh lived for three years on Adak, and neighboring islands taking possession on behalf of the Russian crown. These Andreanof Islands are now called after him. Catherine II gave him the title, "Siberian Noble," and also charged the fur-hunters to treat the natives with kindness, and to avoid all oppression and ill treatment of their new brothers.

Father Jette points out that the Great Tsarina's recommendation was not altogether uncalled for. The Russian traders, especially Glottof and Solovief had been "paving the way" to Christianity with bodies of murdered Aleuts. These natives were friendly at first, but had been worked to exasperation by the Russians, and since 1762 they had been openly hostile, especially on the Islands of Unalaska and Kodiak.

No one knows who gave the first provocation; whether the Russians by oppression, or the Aleuts by refusing to submit. We are told that one winter the Islanders destroyed three Russian ships. In response the Russians, pretending to avenge the blood of their countrymen, adopted stringent measures for their own protection. Glottof destroyed all the villages on the southern side of the Island of Umnak, and the inhabitants of the Islands of Samalgi and Four Mountains. Solovief treated the poor Aleuts of Unalaska with excessive cruelty. Various estimates are given of the number of natives murdered, some historians crediting Solovief with 5,000 deaths.

Veniaminof, the greatest of the Russian missionaries, who became the first Bishop of Russian America, said: "I have personally interviewed many Aleuts who have known Solovief. Though there is no necessity of parading the dreadful cruelties of ignorant and vicious people, especially as these men were Russians and my countrymen, I am compelled to speak of what I heard from very many who had been eye-witnesses or heard the same from Solovief's own companions. This must be done in order to bring forward new evidence of what men will do when left to themselves with unlimited power and no fear of retribution."

Ivan Petrof explains it further in his *Compilation of Narratives of Explorations in Alaska.* He says: "The history of the Russian discoveries for the next twenty years (1762–1782) is a continuous story of outrages committed by the numerous trading expeditions, and of internal quarrels between themselves. The success of the earliest adventurers had been so great that every Siberian merchant who had a few thousand rubles at his command sought to fit out a miserable craft or two, and over sixty distinct enterprises can be traced. These so-called traders had managed to do their business with an exceedingly small stock of goods. Where no opposition was offered by the natives, the invaders did not even pretend to buy skins of them, but forced them to go out and hunt, and turn their booty over to the fur hunters without payment beyond a few beads and a leaf or two of tobacco."

After 1770 the cruelties inflicted upon the natives caused a gradual decrease in the fur supply, and this aroused the suspicions of a Siberian trader, Gregor Shelikof. He organized a company and equipped three ships, two of which reached Unalaska and Kodiak in 1784. Here in addition to his business activities, he baptized the natives.

Petrof says: "He showed them the advantages of living according to the customs of Christianity and civilization, and the poor miserable savages were only too glad to be allowed to partake of such rude comforts as the Russian traders could boast, and in return for these advantages were always willing to go through any

ceremony Shelikof chose to perform. Nearly all the
captives and many of the visitors from the neighboring
tribes and villages were baptized and duly counted as
members of the Orthodox Church."

Father Jette observes that the exercise and claim of
the spiritual jurisdiction by the State and the Russian
Church was plainly a usurpation of the ecclesiastical by
the civil power. Both authorities were vested in the Tsar
who was primarily the political ruler, and only second-
arily the ecclesiastical head of the Russians.

After two years of successful trading Shelikof returned to Sibera with a considerable amount of furs
which were honestly gotten. He sent his maps and
reports, saying that he had gained 50,000 subjects for
the Tsarina, and made three requests: he wanted extensive trading privileges, as well as missionaries and
convicts to accompany him on his next trip. The requests were granted, and his next expedition left
Okhotsk, arriving at Kodiak in the fall of 1794, with
eight missionaries and 200 convicts.

Three years later Shelikof received his patents of
nobility, and a few days afterwards died. However, his
widow and son-in-law, Count Nikolai Rezanof, continued the Shelikof Company. Then appeared the man
who was to control wisely and efficiently the Muscovite
commercial policy for more than twenty-five years. His
name was A. A. Baranov. In 1799 Tsar Paul gave this
Russian American Company a charter which granted it
the exclusive monopoly of trade in Russian America as
well as administration of the islands and adjacent main-

land. Baranov's successors were as incompetent as he
was competent, and it was their continued mistakes that
made Russia welcome the sale of the country to the
United States in 1867.

One notices a rather unhealthy degree of speed in the
work of the first missionaries. For instance, a former
engineer named Juvenal in two years baptized all the
natives in the villages he visited. At length, he met an
untimely death at the hands of the savages because of
his objection to polygamy. Another priest, Makar,
within two years "baptized all the Aleuts, without
exception."

Now as Father Jette remarks, these men took no
time to instruct the people, completely forgetting the
Divine command not only to baptize but to teach. For
this reason their Converts could hardly be considered
Christians. But they became Russian citizens by virtue
of their baptism, and the desire of securing this advantage accounted no doubt for the readiness of their
conversion.

For over fifty years from their entry to Kodiak Island,
the Russian missionaries lived in various stations on the
Aleutian Islands and on the mainland of Alaska. They
built chapels and churches, but their method was always
the same: to baptize and administer the sacraments
without previous instruction. Such then were the beginnings of missionary work in Alaska.

A casual reader may get the impression that Russian
Imperialism on the American Continent lasted through
long periods of time. But, in reality they were short and

belong to our very recent history. The first traders began coming to the Aleutian Islands not long after the middle of the eighteenth century. For forty years the fur trading activity was one unbridled scramble for wealth carried on for the most part by unscrupulous traders. Only in 1799 was the right of political administration given to the Russian American Company. This portion of the Russian occupation continued for only sixty-eight years. Alaska was sold to the United States only seventy-five years ago. American development faces challenging years ahead.

III

The Oblates in Alaska

[1860-1873]

*M*Y FIRST trip to Alaska took me across Canada from Montreal to Prince Rupert. There I providentially met Father Artheme Dutilly, O.M.I. Without the benefit of his profound knowledge as explorer and naturalist of the Oblate missions, and the translation of many unusual sources on the Oblate explorations in Alaska, this chapter would have been even less complete.

A T THE TIME that the United States bought Alaska,
little was known of its vast interior, of the countless miles of wilderness north of the Alaskan
range and west of the Rockies. Only a few journeys of
reconnoitering had been made over the terrain. The
Russian settlements and fur trading activities had, with
few exceptions, been limited to the southern section, the
west coast, and the Aleutian, Kodiak, and a few other
islands. The Hudson's Bay Company's northwest out-
post was Fort Yukon, at the junction of the Porcupine
and Yukon Rivers, and this organization was better
informed of the interior than anyone else. It was a land
drained by the Yukon and its tributaries whose water-
shed climbed up to the Brooks range on the northwest,
and down to the Alaskan range on the southeast. The
villages of the Loucheux (also called Tinnah) Indians
dotted the river banks. These tribes were known for
their intelligent and responsive natures.

Into this forbidding world came the Oblate Missionary Fathers. From their headquarters on the Great
Slave Lake, some two thousand miles southeast of Fort
Yukon in the Northwest Territories, they had already
established missions as far as Good Hope on the Mackenzie River. This point was of the same latitude as
Fort Yukon, and some four hundred and fifty miles
east of it. These geographical notes help to bring out
the great effort and distance involved, and the amount

of hardihood and mettle needed by these explorer-
missionaries.

We first hear of them in 1860 from a letter of Father
Grollier who writes: "If God spares me, I myself intend
to go to the Yukon soon, and even to Alaska through
the forests of Russian America."

Though Arctic travelers use much the same methods
of getting about today as they did in bygone years, yet
the intervening time has done much to ease the effort.
In the early years of exploration, one had either to pack
all the food needed for a long journey, or to live off the
land by hunting and fishing. Although much of the
country is still a solitary expanse, yet the traveler now
finds an occasional roadhouse (hotel) where from time
to time he can add to his supplies of food.

In 1861 Father Grollier set out to reach Fort Yukon.
He wanted to preach the Gospel to the Loucheux Indians, but got only as far as Pierre's House in the middle
of the Rocky Mountains, where he built a little hut in
honor of Saint Barnabas. A missionary rather than an
explorer, it was his desire to stay with the Indians for
all eternity. His bones now lie in the Indian country at
Good Hope.

The following year a more successful missionary en-
terprise was launched when Father Seguin spent the
winter and actually worked among these Indians. He
had left the Peel River, a tributary of the Mackenzie
early in June, 1862, arriving two weeks later at Pierre's
House.

"After a trying march through rugged mountains

and rushing rivers, in addition to having been eaten
alive by swarms of mosquitoes during the whole trip,"
he reached Fort Yukon three months later. The difficulty of word-painting the hardships and trials of these
men is obvious. Not that the missionaries were the only
men who bore them. The early traders gave up the
comforts of civilization and faced unknown hardships,
and so did the miners. But, the motives of their conduct
were poles apart. The missionaries wanted to carry out
Christ's command of preaching the gospel to all men.
The traders and miners wanted Gold.

This is the first time that a Catholic priest had appeared in this region, and though twelve or thirteen
hundred Indians lived in the vicinity of the fort, only
about forty of them had assembled at the missionary's
arrival. The others, scattered over the woods, were not
expected until the spring. And so, Father Seguin waited
for them.

Father Duchaussois in his book, *Mid Snow and Ice,*
recounts that Father Seguin was then twenty-eight
years of age. Though accustomed only to his books,
he managed to become artisan, carpenter, clockmaker,
painter and sculptor, and put Father Grollier's hut into
a state of good repair. But his life at the fort these winter
months was not a pleasant one. The chief trader of the
post did not approve of Catholic activities, and would
encourage nothing that might foster them. While he
shared his table with the Anglican minister, he relegated
the Oblate father to the servants' quarters for meals and
lodging. The humiliation as such meant nothing to

Father Seguin. The effect of this social snub, however, on his relations with the Indians was damaging. Accustomed as they were to judge by appearances, they reasoned that this must be a poor specimen of preacher, and refused to come to listen to him. Another great obstacle with which the Oblate missionary had to contend was the language difficulty. An interpreter named Houle, instead of translating the priest's message of the gospel, gave the Indians his own version; he pointed out to his audience that there was really no need to give up polygamy as the Catholic religion insisted they must do. This combination of adverse circumstances made the missionary's task a very difficult one.

During the following spring Father Seguin made a number of journeys into the Indian country and worked among the Loucheux. Once on arriving at Pierre's House, he wrote to his novice master:

"When I arrived here my head was like a gourd, and my fingers like sausages. If you have any novices longing for mortification, send them out here where hardships are plentiful every day of the year."

With the coming of June he set out eastward through the yet half frozen streams. Here we must diverge to explain a peculiar situation which takes place in this section where the rivers flow from south to north into the Arctic Ocean. They are frozen solid through the winter, and begin the spring thaw first in the south, whereupon the flow of water rushes north into a section of the river which is still frozen. This is especially terrific at the ramparts where the narrow river is confined between steep walls. When the great floods of spring are obliged to pass through these narrow confines, the ice keeps slipping, one layer over the other, making a dam. Sometimes the jam of ice assumes fantastic shapes, and reaches a height of seventy feet. When the weather relents and these jams give way, the force of the scraping ice often shaves off the trees high above the shore line.

Such was the wild kind of world these explorer missionaries had to face, and not knowing what to expect, they found it doubly difficult.

Seven years elapsed before the arrival of another Oblate. In the summer of 1870 Reverend Emile Petitot reached the Yukon.

He was a great explorer, and archeologist, and used to walk through the country gun in hand, dressed as an Eskimo and living entirely off the land. He was also a scientist, writer and a pioneer in the Innuit language. He had a good ear and could take down the sentences and words he heard when he had nothing to base the sounds on. He was important as a historian as well. At that time a scientific convention in Paris was trying to disprove the unity of the human race. One premise was that the primitive American did not come from Asia or Europe, but was indigenous to the American continent. Emile Petitot told the scientists of the thousand-mile trips the Eskimo had made along the Arctic coast in the summer. If they could do this, he pointed out, certainly they could have come from Asia even in the earlier days when the Bering Strait was wider.

This kind of controversy seems strange to the twentieth century, but in the eighteen hundreds, there were believers for both sides of the question. Father Petitot had also made a thorough study of Eskimo folklore. Through it he traced their idea of good and evil, of a supreme being. The Eskimo versions were greatly embellished with trappings, but they still contained the essence of such stories as the deluge, and Adam and Eve. With this logic he helped to show his case that the Eskimo derived from an older race, and did not begin on the American continent. This he did in Paris. In Alaska he stayed but a short time.

He was followed by Bishop Isidore Clut, who during this period of Oblate exploration did more comprehensive work than anyone. He considered that the country was a neutral region, and under no settled spiritual direction. He decided that the natives of Alaska were his responsibility, and set out from Good Hope September 14, 1872, with Father August Lecorre and a young Hare Indian. Bishop Clut was a noble figure, fully six feet in height, with a large flowing beard. They descended the Mackenzie to the mouth of the Peel, and a short journey up this river brought them to the Hudson's Bay Company's trading post of Fort McPherson. They were five days in making the portage to Pierre's House on Rat River West. There they obtained an old skin canoe in which they journeyed down the winding stream to the Porcupine River. But in this river, ice was already forming along the shores and large floes were soon drifting with the stream. The ice overtook them, the river jammed, and they were obliged to halt until it closed. For a pleasing description of part of this journey I am indebted to Father Jette's *The Jottings of an Alaskan Missionary,* which he wrote in the years around 1909 while working with the Tinnah Indians on the middle Yukon.

"These last warm days of the arctic autumn were just over and the winter was coming at great strides. Yellowed by the first touches of the frost, leaves of willows and cotton trees dropped and whirled with every gust of the breeze, and were swept along the rushing waters which were now confined to their narrowest channels. Here and there broad expanses of mud-bars and cow-banks just bared by the retiring stream added a dingy feature to the gloomy scene. The ice-cold water soon covered the oar-blades with a glossy sheet of ice, which thickened at every dip. Soon it grew to a heavy icicle which they would stop to break now and then.

"Migrating birds, ducks of many kinds, geese, black, white and grey, cranes and snow-white swans hovered overhead in long, geometrically drawn lines, speeding south. With them the last cheering feature was departing from the freezing landscape. Snow was falling. All this told the travelers of coming hardships and privations; and as there was no doubt in their minds as to its meaning, there was no hesitation in their hearts."

Bishop Clut stood the journey better than Father Lecorre, who was still suffering from a kind of Paris green poisoning, the result of an Indian's carelessness in

cleaning a copper kettle. Time was too precious to allow
of a halt even for a sick man. While the river ice was
forming, they constructed a rough sled, and as soon as
they could travel again, set out for the west. It took
them eight days to reach Fort Yukon. The unexpected
delay caused their provisions to give out, and they
reached the Post in an exhausted condition, just a
month after leaving Good Hope.

The stockaded post of Fort Yukon had already been
deserted by the Hudson's Bay Company since it was
now United States territory. The missionaries found
there an entirely sympathetic staff headed by Moses
Mercier.

The seven months they remained at Fort Yukon were
not marked by success in preaching the gospel to the
Indians. Only a few of them came to the religious services. Father Lecorre in visiting the natives of Nulato
said he was delighted to find he could converse with
them, as there was but a slight difference between their
idiom and that of the Mackenzie tribes.

As soon as the ice broke in May the missionaries left
for their long exploratory trip down the Yukon, just as
the first four prospectors for gold, who were to be followed by such a host of others, arrived at Fort Yukon.
Bishop Clut and his companions stopped at Nukluroyit,
an Indian village near where Fort Gibbon and later
Tanana was to be built. There they taught the word of
God to the natives who had gathered in great numbers
for the spring trading. A Pontifical high mass was celebrated in front of the cabin on the high river bank of

the Yukon in the presence of hundreds of natives and whites.

In June the two missionaries accompanied Francis Mercier, a brother of the Fort Yukon agent, to St. Michael. Besides the two missionaries and the agent, the boat was loaded with furs, and stopped at every village along the river. One hundred and sixteen babies were baptized on that trip. After a three weeks' stay Bishop Clut went up the Yukon and back to his Vicariate while Father Lecorre stayed until the spring. A great part of the winter he spent working among the natives at St. Michael and around the sea shore. By January his supplies began to ebb. Part of the time he had to live in his little cabin and subsist mainly on slap-jacks. To add to his difficulties, what was left of his stock of altar wine was so little that he could not continue to say his daily mass.

The expedition of Bishop Clut and Father Lecorre was the last attempt of the Oblate Fathers to evangelize Alaska. By dint of great toil and hardship, a noble beginning had been made. It was to be continued by the Jesuits under Bishop Seghers to whom Propaganda now assigned Alaska. The Oblates spread their missions among the Eskimo far up into the Arctic regions, but the Mackenzie River flowing into the Arctic now became their western terminus.

IV
Archbishop Seghers
[1877-1886]

FROM Bishop Crimont's own lips I first heard the story of Archbishop Seghers, the great Alaskan adventurer of whom I knew nothing before. I marveled that one with such a life should be so little known outside ecclesiastical circles. Though more than half a century has passed since his death, the first biography of him in America is now being brought out. It is a translation by Mother Mildred Welsh, S.S.A. of Maurice De Baets' Vie de Msgr. Seghers.

"WISDOM REACHETH from end to end mightily and ordereth all things sweetly." Certainly Bishop Charles John Seghers must have found it difficult to understand the divine order of things when, on returning from his first long trip to Alaska, he found he had been named Coadjutor Archbishop of Oregon. The transfer from his post in Victoria to his new one as Archbishop of the rangy Oregon territory was a great honor, but it meant giving up his plans for Alaska, and this he could not help regretting. Alaska had been bought by the United States only eleven years before, and Rome had now made it a part of the diocese of Vancouver Island. The challenge of exploring its vast interior and working with the Eskimo and Indians meant much to him. His dream of the far north had become almost an obsession, and suddenly he had to give it up.

Having spent the previous winter with the Indians at Nulato and learned their language with ease, he had lost his heart to the country. He had also visited the Koyukuk River, the Unalakleet portage, and the villages as far southwest along the Yukon as Russian Mission. Before the ice broke the following spring, he and his companion, Father Mandart, went up to Nukluroyit and after working for six weeks among the natives there, returned by barge to St. Michael, thence to San Francisco. He had only just stepped off the boat when the news of his transfer crashed down on him.

We are told he gave up his plans with holy resignation, but we can picture him spending a few reluctant moments on his way to appoint missionaries at Sitka and Wrangell. Then he began his work in Oregon, at which point his name appeared likely to drop out of the history of Alaska.

Oregon at this time was a very young country. Some thirty-three years before, when its territory was detached from Quebec and made a Vicariate Apostolic, Oregon City had only a few more than sixty houses. A year later, in 1845, the boundary was settled, and Oregon was established as a United States possession.

Archbishop Seghers' activity there, however, was not destined to last long, for in 1883 his plans were changed for him again. With the other Archbishops of the country, he was called to Rome to make preparations for the Plenary Council of Baltimore. While there he conferred with Cardinal Simeoni, who was concerned about appointing a new man to the See of Victoria. Bishop Brondel had been transferred from there to Helena, Montana, leaving Archbishop Seghers' old post vacant.

When the Cardinal spoke of his concern over a new appointee, Archbishop Seghers looked at him in amazement. As though there could be more than one solution to that problem:

"Let me be sent back to Victoria, Your Eminence," he cried. "I shall take care of Alaska."

This meant giving up his important Oregon diocese and returning to the smaller one from which he had been canonically elevated. But such a demotion meant nothing to him. On his way back, he lectured in his fur parka in Belgium, and all the way across the United States, in behalf of the Alaskan missions.

Back in Victoria, he lost little time in planning another expedition, and in 1886, with two Jesuit Fathers of the Rocky Mountain Province, Pascal Tosi and Aloysius Robaut, he made his fifth and last trip to Alaska. Frank Fuller, a jack-of-all-trades, was employed to assist in the venture. Though he was helpful in many ways, he was afflicted with a persecution mania which increased with the hardships of the trip.

One of the Archbishop's letters describes their journey through Miles Canyon and White Horse Canyon.

"One boat was unloaded and the cargo packed across the trail along the canyon. Brother Fuller took the helm, Father Robaut took one oar, and the miner took the other, and as I did not want to see my people jeopardize their lives without sharing their danger, I took my place in the front of the boat, my watch in hand, to measure the velocity of our locomotion. We started off at 1 P.M. and in a moment the swift current caught our boat and whirled it between the breakers on each side of the canyon. It was a terrible scene. We were visibly on an incline, rushing down hill with the velocity of a locomotive. The roaring of the water, the spray that filled the air all around us, the waves that struck our scow, which rolled and pitched as on the billows of the sea, made an impression on our minds that will not easily be forgotten. But we had no time for reflection. In a few minutes we found ourselves in a slack current and

between two eddies which we had to avoid most carefully. Then another plunge into the rest of the canyon
. . . finally we emerged from the dark place, having made a mile in three minutes and twenty-five seconds."

They climbed and struggled through country which was then an absolute wilderness. After many narrow escapes from the jaws of death, they at length reached the mouth of the Stewart River. There the missionaries separated. The two priests remained at the camp with the miners, and Archbishop Seghers and Fuller continued down the river, planning to spend the rest of the winter with the Indians at Nulato. At the end of four weeks they reached Nukluroyit on the middle Yukon where they spent considerable time. From this point on, the missionary's diary contains some ominous entries. One note says:

"Curious conversation with Fuller who gives for the third time proofs of his insanity." At another time— "The brother is angry at breakfast: he accuses me of wanting to ruin him."

It was probably with great joy that the Archbishop found himself once more on the middle Yukon with the Indians whose language he had mastered and who were devoted to him. Nine years had passed since he had seen them last. The interregnum in Oregon and his trip to Europe were but distant memories. He was back with his beloved Indians: he would spend the rest of his life working for, and as much as possible, among them. So he proposed.

But God disposed. He was to give his life for the

evangelization of these, his people, but the details were not to be as he had sketched them. They were drawn in quick, sharp, stark lines. He had planned to give his whole lifetime, but now he was asked to give his life, and that immediately. He yearned for service, God demanded sacrifice.

It was almost the end of November and the Missionary, Fuller and two Indians plodded over the snow from Nukluroyit to an Indian cabin a day's journey from Nulato, where they spent the night. Long before daybreak, Fuller left the cabin on the pretext of getting some fuel. On returning a few minutes later he carried his gun. He threw some bark on the fire, and shouted:

"Bishop, get up."

The Archbishop sat up on the bearskin which had been his blanket, and seeing the gun leveled at him, bowed his head, crossed his arms on his breast, and in an attitude of resignation, received his death wound. So it is that the early morning of November 27, 1886 is the real beginning of Alaska's permanent missions. The seed was nourished in blood and signed with the seal of the Cross.

The Jesuit Order magnificently continued the work entrusted them by Propaganda of founding the Alaska missions, first in the persons of Father Tosi and Father Robaut, and beginning with Holy Cross and the missions along the middle Yukon. Shortly after, a mission began on the Yukon Delta where in 1891 Francis Barnum was sent as missionary and linguist.

V

Beginnings on the Yukon Delta

[1891-1894]

THE READER will remember meeting Father Barnum at the boat at St. Michael when Father Crimont made his first voyage to Alaska. Practically all of our knowledge of the beginnings on the Yukon Delta comes from his two books and letters which are alive with good humor.

Someone told me that his conversion began when he was a young man on his way home from Europe. A fellow-passenger hurled out of the door of his cabin a copy of Cardinal Gibbons' Faith of Our Fathers, and Francis Barnum happened along in time to pick it up.

IN EARLY YEARS the Alaskan missionaries had a very easy way of renewing their annual supplies. They simply wrote a letter to their procurator in San Francisco. Ordinarily three steamers plied every year between San Francisco and the interior, so that the shipping of supplies was none too difficult a problem. The freight for the Coast Mission arrived on the freighter which brought Joseph Raphael Crimont, and Father Francis Barnum tarried only a day before boating it along the coast to his mission. For the benefit of the new missionary, he filled the interval with the narrative in his jocular and graphic manner of the beginnings in great poverty of the Catholic missions on the Yukon Delta. Father Barnum had traveled widely, and his study for the priesthood had not damped, but rather quickened his great fund of wit and charm.

When he came to Alaska three years earlier, the Jesuit missions were already stretched from Nukluroyit on the middle Yukon southwest along the river to the Bering Sea. This was no small effort for so short a time, and with so few workers. The Coast Mission to which Father Barnum was sent was on a bleak, blizzard-swept island consisting of long stretches of tundra partially protected by a range of volcanic hills. It was just opposite Nunivak Island which can be easily located on the map.

The great spring freshets of the Yukon and Kuskokwim Rivers carrying down immense quantities of driftwood, determined the location of the Eskimo villages. Since there were no trees about, the rivers became the source of building material. And the grouping of these native communities some forty miles distant from each other along the coast made the section a logical one for the missionaries to choose.

The first loghouse of the Coast Mission had served many purposes and seems to have been an object of great curiosity. Father Tosi, then head of the missions, had been its architect and master workman. Father Treca functioned as consulting engineer, log roller and cook. The result of their combined efforts, impeded by several good-natured natives, came to be the extraordinary domicile which Father Barnum described as a cross between an old Virginia smoke-house, a Harlem shanty, and a native barrabora.

The only building material available was the drift wood washed along the coast by the various currents of the sea. The plans called for a structure eighteen feet wide by twenty feet long. It seems that two sides of the house agreed with the measurements of the original design, but the other two differed just enough to make one gable lean inward and the corresponding one outward. For this reason four large props were required to hold the building upright. No one was able to determine the front of the house for there was no clue to it, the entrance being merely a side door.

The edifice was built of forty logs, ten layers high, the space between the logs being caulked with moss.

Sometimes when the rain poured, the moss would loosen and fall to the ground, resulting in an onrush of cold air like steam from a boiler. The roof was composed of split logs laid close together.

The interstices were packed with straw, the whole surface being covered with tarred paper, over which was placed a covering of sod, and finally a thick layer of earth in which every luxuriant vegetation of spring grew. In spite of the immense weight of this roof, the furious winter gales fairly toppled the little shanty; often too, because of its exposed position along the coast, it became so completely buried in snow that the Fathers could not make an exit until the natives came and disinterred them.

The interior of the dwelling was divided into two unequal compartments by a piece of old sailcloth. The larger section was the Basilica of Saint Alfonso, the other, the Superior's room. Since this contained a small cooking stove, it served at once as kitchen, refectory, and recreation room. Moreover, its one shelf of books, and its other shelf containing caster-oil and a jar of pills, ranked it as a library and pharmacy. Up above was a little cockloft scarcely high enough to allow a man to stand upright; here, among the provisions, Brother Cunningham and Father Barnum had their bunks.

The crowning glory of the cabin, Father Barnum explained, was its great west window—the handiwork of Father Treca—fashioned after an antique model. Six photographic plates, their film scraped off, had been inserted into the curiously wrought frame. However, as Father Barnum pointed out, windows were of no use whatever on the Bering Sea. In summer they were not needed; in winter one could not see through them, for nearly an inch of solid ice formed on the inside, exactly as if extra panes of ground glass were set in the sash. The icy curtain not only helped to chill the room, but rendered the glass so opaque that those inside could scarcely distinguish day from night.

The general aspect of the country along the Bering Sea was not alluring, since it was entirely devoid of trees, and intersected by innumerable rivers. Their deposits of silt had made the sea so shallow that for miles from the shore there was not water enough at low tide to launch a row-boat. The whole country was vol canic, with immense lava beds and extinct craters on every side. Between the rivers were interminable wet plains called tundra by the Russians, which meant that the sub-soil was frozen. A thick growth of moss, covering the land, held so much water that travelling over it, except during the winter, was almost impossible.

"All that you can see from our Mission," Father Barnum said, "is the cold grey sea, with a cold grey stretch of country, covered by a cold grey sky. All that you hear about Alaska's wonderful scenery, its glaciers and its volcanoes, has no meaning up here. That's true of the southeastern part, but this is an entirely different region.

"During a part of the year, the mosquito plague makes many villages uninhabitable. This is especially true in the delta of the Yukon, and leading a nomadic life becomes a stern necessity to the Eskimo. Naturally since the missionaries must go to the natives, fixing a mission location is indeed a difficult undertaking."

Father Barnum's analysis of the weather was vivid. In summer, he said, there was a great amount of fog, while the dreariest feature of the winter was the darkness. However, the cold was dry and intense, and on a dry day one could go out-of-doors without discomfort. During the winter months the long, gloomy hours from two in the afternoon until ten in the morning made a long and monotonous night, while most of the days were so cloudy that a lamp was needed. Terrific blizzards, lasting from three to five days, occurred almost weekly. At such times it was dangerous to venture out-of-doors. In March the radiance of the sun increased. That, too, was not without its disadvantages, for the glare of the sun produced snow blindness which was extremely painful. Sometimes after a trip the Fathers would be laid up for several days until the inflammation around their eyes had subsided.

One added horror was yet to be explained, and that was a subject on which little had to be said.

"When I first landed at St. Michaels three years ago," Father Barnum said, "we camped on the bluff for two weeks while the steamer discharged cargo. Soon I noticed a little rash which broke out on my neck."

He told how with great difficulty he refrained from scratching until the boat had left, since he was afraid his superior might send him back for complaining. But one day he had to rub a speck on the shoulder of his coat and Father Tosi, head of the missions, calmly re-marked. "So you have gotten some already."

Father Barnum said it required constant vigilance to keep free from the louse. "Every time you enter a casine, you get a fresh supply. When you visit the sick or come in contact with the people in any way, you are bound to catch them."

The Eskimo's dress, which consisted of a fur parka and a pair of long boots, was never subjected to the ordeal of the wringer and mangle. On occasions, how-ever, the clothes would be hung outside until they froze; then as many insects as possible would be shaken off.

His gloomy description was not an exaggerated ac-count given for the instruction of his new confrere, for it accorded with the reality. Yet, the twinkle in his eye made it evident that the lack of creature comforts made no difference at all to his enjoyment of the work. He had come to Alaska as a linguist and scholar, and in addition to the heavy mission work, he was making a systematic study of Eskimo language. This kind of re-search, with the production of an Innuit Grammar, was naturally very different from picking up the vernacular by daily converse with the Eskimo. A few other Eskimo dictionaries had been compiled, based on the idioms in use in other sections of the north. But no attempt had as yet been made to systematize the dialect used along the Bering Sea. Farther Barnum described his method of going about the work.

"Suppose," he said, "you are in a boat, you pick up an oar, point to it and say 'Cha'—what? The native gazes placidly at you and says 'Chuya-ugeeakoa.'

"You write the native word carefully in your note-book, and feel that you have a start, and so you endeavor to obtain the verb. Therefore, you row a few strokes, and then you 'cha' (what?) again. Probably by this time he is sulky at not receiving any tobacco, or he is suspicious over the mysterious activity of the pencil, so he pays no further attention to you. But if he is a very intelligent fellow, he will say 'Thou hast been rowing.'

"Splendid, down it goes in the note-book, but you notice with a degree of disappointment that there is no similarity between the two words. Next you point to a native who is rowing near you, and 'cha.' But you get no place with this.

"Next you say, 'How do you say—I row?'

"He may here suppose you wish a friendly criticism on your stroke, and with native simplicity says:

" 'Thou rowest very poorly.'

"At the end of your effort, your note-book looks something like this:

"Oar—I would like some tobacco.
  1st person singular:—Thou rowest very poorly.
  2nd person singular:—What do you want?
  3rd person singular:—You both are rowing.
  1st person plural:— Ye row.
  2nd person plural:— Thou hast been rowing.
  3rd person plural:— We are tired of rowing.

"After considerable research you discover that the word for oar is chavuetet, not chuya-ugeeakoa. Then the whole tense is laboriously reconstructed."

VI

Bishop Crimont, Early Years

[1858-1894]

*W*ITHOUT *a journal to use as a skeleton, it was difficult for Bishop Crimont to travel down the years of memory. And a strong theory grew within me that missionaries should be taught to keep diaries. As this book is finished the theory is solidified into a conviction. Future historians of missionary outposts might not be endowed by God with the sleuth-like patience, in addition to a traveling job which enabled me to collect the material for* Dogsled Apostles.

There was information that probably would have died with its author if I had not the good fortune of finding it when I did: letters rich in detail that would never have been written had I not kept after their authors for the facts: humble people who would have carried to the graves their glorious adventures with God had I not been sent to them.

And so, on the other hand, if all this mission material had been codified and edited, I would never have known the charming friends whose lives and ideas fill these pages. Perhaps my solid conviction about the keeping of diaries should revert to tentative theory again.

THERE IS A MYSTERY in the life of Bishop Joseph Raphael Crimont which challenges his friends. His physical condition for many years was a wavering trail of weakness. He was so delicate during his childhood and youth that his Superiors were convinced he would die young. In his middle twenties he was so ill he was not expected to live more than a few weeks. Yet at the grand old age of eighty-four, he is still alive, adding to the forty-five years of his toiling in rugged Alaska.

The spiritual vitality shining through his life has produced a record of steady and heroic achievements. Amid the rigors of the country, he has stood the hard work of shepherding his scattered flock, meanwhile outliving all his contemporary missionaries. One might be led to imagine a man of iron frame and sturdy appearance. In reality he is a man of slender build, slight of appearance, short of stature. And withal, his features are delicate.

Joseph Raphael Crimont was born February 2, 1858, in Ferrieres, near Amiens in the north of France, where his ancestors had been as long as could be remembered. Here he lived his first three years with his father, his mother, two brothers, and two sisters.

His father was a coupeur de velours which meant he earned his living by making cotton velvet, a product for which Amiens had been famous since the middle ages.

He would bring home the unworked cloth from the manufacturer in Amiens, and his skilled hands would run the sharp knife over the cloth cutting the loops of soft thread. This was one stage toward making the finished product. And in this he labored until the last years of his life, when he could work no more.

The small wages for this work enforced extreme thrift, and sometimes real hardship, on the families of these craftsmen. The house of Ferrieres in which Joseph was born was a one-story adobe structure with a thatched roof. Now after eighty-four years, its type can no longer be found either in the country or village. The living room had an open fireplace in which slow-burning peat produced a steady temperature during night and day, and took away the dampness from the bare ground. The storeroom for provision came next, and after that the workroom of the senior Joseph Crimont, who could be heard singing hymns while he was cutting the threads of cloth. Next came the family's sleeping quarters.

At the back of the house was a garden plot with cabbage, turnips, potatoes, lettuce and onions. This rather limited food supply was augmented from a farm in which Alexandrine Niquet Crimont had inherited part interest, and which, among other things, produced the oil used for the Crimont table. The young family drank a good deal of goat milk and caught a few rabbits, but it was difficult to supply from the garden all the necessary food. After more than eighty years the Bishop can still remember the family's joy when friends contributed a few eggs to be roasted in the embers of the Crimont fireplace. Quite often for a meal they had only a piece of bread with vinegar, oil and an onion, and the Bishop says that the scarcity of more nourishing food stunted his growth and kept him from developing into a larger man.

When Joseph was three the family moved to Amiens, for his father, always a devout man, reasoned in this way:

"God may have some designs on this family. If we stay in this village the children will have no chance for education and training." There was another advantage to the move, for it did away with the long trips to and from the Amiens manufacturer.

In Amiens they lived in the country near the edge of town, in the Vincentian Parish of St. Anne. On trips to the town market, we can picture his mother hurrying along the broad boulevard lined with chestnut and lime trees, Joseph toddling by her side and being carried when he was tired. Sometimes when the hedgebanks were yellow with primroses they would go into the country and watch the shaggy sheepdogs. But this life did not last long, for a great tragedy came to them. Cholera was spreading desolation over the whole continent, and in its path lay Amiens in the north of France. People left their homes to go shopping, but Death overtook them on the way. Some were taken with the disease on the street and were removed to the hospital; others fell dead. The plague crept to the doorstep of the Crimont home and attacked Alexandrine Niquet Crimont, Joseph's mother. She was carried to the hospital and died, while Joseph's younger brother, with a slighter case, was nursed back to health at home.

The children were then sent to the country to escape the epidemic, and lived with their Aunts Veronica and Sidonie: Joseph used to walk to town with them each month when they attended the Third Order of Franciscan meetings. They did not speak customary French, but a special Picardy language. Amiens had always been the chief town of the old province of Picardy. After the French Revolution the name of the province was changed to the Department of Sommes. In this peasant language the boy's pet name was Chaufa. "Chau" was patois for "petit" and was combined with the second syllable of his name, Raphael.

One of the picturesque memories of his childhood was the sight of his Uncle Lopite, a tall man who was the Suisse in church. In his uniform of red coat, large buttons, high hat, knee pants, and lance, he was both usher and policeman, and could control any situation: when there was a procession he marched like a drum major before it. Often when a dog came into the church during the services, the priest would cry loudly to him: "Herald of Helvetia—drive away that symbol of infidelity."

When Joseph was six, the family returned to Amiens, and he attended kindergarten, then public school, and at seven, he was placed with his elder brother in a charitable boarding school. At the age of ten he attended St. Martin's, a school for boys who seemed to have a vocation. His talent was not long in making itself ob-

served. When he was eleven he attended the Apostolic
School in Amiens, just established by Father F. X.
Barbelin, S.J. Its object was the training of boys who
showed vocations, no matter what religious order they
intended to join. After Joseph's First Communion at the
end of that year, he and two other boys were recommended for La Providence, the Jesuit school in Amiens.

Father Barbelin in presenting them, said: "Of course
Maes and Grisbach are all right: they seem to have
good health, but as for little Crim, I don't know. He has
very little health, but he has the stuff to become a saint.
Anyhow, if he does not live long, he may try to imitate
St. Stanislaus."

So, little Crim was told to pray that he might live
long enough to take his vows as a religious. Meanwhile
he went from La Providence to St. Acheul, the Jesuit
House of Studies at Amiens, which had been a monas-
tery before the French Revolution. But now came the
time when his life was despaired of.

It was in his first year of philosophy and the Jesuits
were being expelled from France. The young novices
from St. Acheul were first moved to Boulogne and a few
months later to Louvain, where in September of 1882
Joseph Crimont was ordained subdeacon. A rude shock
lay in store for him. His health was so bad that he could
not stay in school. At the time the doctors were discussing his condition with the Father Superior, it happened
that Madame De Coster was bringing back to school
her Jesuit son after nursing him through a siege of
typhoid fever. When she heard that Joseph Crimont

was ill, she offered to take this delicate student to her home and try to restore him to health too. So it was that the middle of the school year found Joseph Crimont living with the De Coster family in Lille.

His sickness was not a sudden thing: the anemic condition was long in coming. It was no doubt the rigors of his ascetic discipline during the first years of his religious life that helped to bring him to the gates of death. Sometimes he had periods of insomnia lasting over a month, and along with it neuralgic headaches. But through it all he was very happy, and was consumed with the love of God.

After another thorough examination, the doctor's verdict came, and it had the effect of a hard blow. To say his life was despaired of was an understatement. He was given two or three weeks to live. The De Coster family was deeply religious and the sharing of his sad plight with them softened its sting. There seemed no hope for the young scholastic, yet help was to come from an entirely unexpected quarter. Don Bosco was coming to Lille to establish an institute for poor boys, and while in the city would stay at St. Joseph's, the Jesuit house. Don Bosco, Apostle of Youth and founder of the Salesian Order, was already known for his miracles. His arrival was of course the talk of the town.

Sympathy perhaps for one with so little time to live, caused the Superior to appoint the young scholastic as one of the servers for Don Bosco's mass. In the sacristy afterwards, Joseph Crimont said to the Saint:

"Father Bosco, I have a great favor to ask of you."

"What is it, my son, if I can do it I shall be so happy."

Then Joseph Crimont told him of his ambition to become a missionary, and of the doctor's verdict that there was no hope for him.

"You obtain from God all that you ask. Would you please ask that I live to be a missionary?"

"Yes, my son. Your ambition will be fulfilled. Every day in my thanksgiving after mass I shall ask God to grant that favor. You will obtain it." And the following year he was again back at the house of studies. The intercession of Don Bosco, however, did not produce a sudden change in the health and fortunes of the young scholastic. It changed the immediate course of the doctor's verdict, but there were yet a few hurdles to cross which threatened the fulfillment of his life's work. However, all this time in his own mind there were no questions: he was going to be a missionary. It was in Liege that his desire took definite shape and set his mind in the direction of North America. Archbishop Charles Seghers had just been reappointed to the See of Victoria which administered the Alaska missions. The Archbishop stopped at Liege on his way from Rome to his native city, Ghent, in the province of East Flanders. He was a brilliant man and a good speaker, and his presence at the school stirred the group of students who heard him. Francis Monroe, who played a large part in Alaskan mission history, was with Joseph Crimont in this group.

Later Father Cataldo, Provincial of the Rocky Mountain missions, came to Europe to recruit young priests for the work, and Joseph Crimont and five others offered themselves. When the Jesuit Provincial visited the school and looked over the list of young men, he gave his consent for five, but crossed out the name of Crimont.

"You cannot make a missionary," he objected. "You are too weak."

"Well, if God wills it," the young priest said, "He will make me one."

"Yes, if He wills it," the Provincial agreed. "But He will have to show me if He wants it."

It was Holy Thursday and Joseph Crimont spent some hours of that day in the chapel.

"I told Our Lord that I wouldn't go away until He told me that I could have my vocation to the Rocky Mountain Mission. Then I prayed and prayed until I thought everything was settled."

And evidently it was settled, for the Provincial gave his consent, and in 1886 Joseph Crimont came to America, where he was ordained by Cardinal Gibbons two years later. He had convinced his superiors that he should be allowed to work on the missions. It never occurred to him that the work might be too hard for him. There was always the quiet confidence that once there, he would find the strength. His life proved that his confidence was justified. The next few years his activity included two trips to Europe, tertianship at Tronchiennes near Ghent, and two years as missionary to the Crow Indians in Montana. Which brings us to 1894 and his first trip to Alaska.

VII
Up the Yukon
[1894]

I FIRST *understood last summer why so few people in the United States have traveled on the lower Yukon. Both its distance and out-of-the-wayness limit visitors. If you start from Seattle you can go by boat via Dutch Harbor and St. Michael, as young Father Crimont did; or you might take the inside passage by boat to Seward, thence by rail to Nenana, then wait for the semi-monthly government freight boat to carry you down the river. The third choice was to go by plane, and this I did.*

Father Crimont's first trip up the lower Yukon took him through a region scarcely touched by the breath of civilization. When I reached there I could see practically nothing that was different from his description of the early years.

THE WOOD-BURNING STEAMBOAT commanded by Captain Healy, an experienced river-boat captain, started happily up the Yukon. Mr. and Mr. Patrick Galvin and Joseph Raphael Crimont were the only through passengers, although natives and a few traders made short journeys along the river. After his enforced fast and confinement most of the way from Seattle to St. Michael, Father Crimont now enjoyed the open space of the boat and with his companions helped himself to the food in the pantry.

The terrain was new to him and he stayed on deck all through the long days watching the muddy Yukon and the Captain maneuvering the boat from one edge of the river to the other, avoiding the newly built sand bars and shallow bottoms. The Yukon was then, as it is now, a fickle river. From year to year, it could be depended on to swerve from side to side, now tearing down the clay banks on the right and building up on the left. It is the largest river in Alaska, and fifth in size of the North American rivers. Its direction too is strange. It flows northwest as far as the Arctic Circle where it turns to the west, then to the southwest for some 500 miles where it empties itself, via four mouths, into the Bering Sea.

Certainly it must have been a great trial to the early Russians who charted it. Baron von Wrangle, the first Russian Governor of Alaska, was responsible for the earliest exploration of the lower Yukon, and his men went northeast until they met the English of the Hudson's Bay Company who were pushing farther and farther west in search of furs.

The river boat passengers watched the great clouds of wild geese and ducks and swans departing for a warmer clime. On the first clear calm days of sailing it was cool, and the fluffy, woolly white clouds were perched far above the horizon to the east. Many of the following days, however, brought steady, continuous downpours of rain.

This was the beginning of fall in this far north country, and the sun had already begun to swing southward. The foliage was becoming tinted with gold, the air was fragrant with a musky-spruce aroma and the odor of wild berries so abundant in the hills. As evening came the murky waters reflected a faint spectrum of color from the heavens as the cumulus clouds floated like kernels of popcorn.

The sunsets offered profuse beauty: the bright gold would turn to a delicate orange, then to a warm cerise, until finally the golden orb sank below the far horizon and a deep greenish purple began to take over the sky. It was an ever-changing study in pastel shades. Sometimes, the travelers rose in the early morning to watch the play of colors: they saw the trees coming to life in the distance, the soft drab gray fused with faint blue and soft pink, while above, the flying mare-tail clouds swung high in the azure sky. Then to the north the colors changed. The reds disappeared and the bright yellows with them. The orange shot out like beams from a gigantic searchlight, breaking through the mystic sweep of the horizon. Again, the colors changed from red to orange to gold; then the great sun appeared suddenly riding the furthest peak, while the chug-chug, splash-splash of the river boat pushed forward to the new day.

Not many days passed before they were beyond the barren, flat delta country. Slowly the river banks changed. Instead of only an abundance of goose grass and moss and scraggy bushes, they saw a few trees, and with them a rise in the land which undulated here and there. The country on the south bank was flat and wooded and to the north the terrain became hilly. Further on could be seen the low peaks, some still angular, others worn smooth and round.

As they plied their way upstream they frequently saw not far from the shore evidences of mining, then in its crude stage. Though the Russians had already operated in this area, only the coarse nuggets were obtained, leaving the richest fine particles behind. Even in the nineties, before the Klondike district brought its thousands of prospectors to the north, there were individuals digging and panning gold without machinery. Sometimes when the boat stopped at the little villages to exchange freight, or along the river's edge to give the crew time to cut the dried driftwood, the travelers came on to a prospector getting the placer gold which had been laid down in the ancient beds of the streams.

Cheerfully the miner would call a "Hallo" that would reverberate along the river. He would be shoveling into

the flume or cradle rocker as he sluiced away the dirt
and rocks to find the precious metal. This was Father
Crimont's first acquaintance with miners. Some ten
and fifteen years later he was destined to know them
considerably better, at his post in the Tanana Valley
district.

Soon a great arm of the river came into view which
the Captain called Portage Slough. Here the native and
white man travel some twenty miles away from the
Yukon, then pack their boat a few miles and arrive in
the Kuskokwim valley with a good navigable stretch of
water. Soon they rounded the bend, and saw a golden
dome amid a cluster of log cabins. This was Russian
Mission, one of the largest settlements on the lower
Yukon, the center of trading for white and native.

The early Russian traders had made their headquarters there and the people had built a beautiful church
of timbers sawed by hand. After weathering the storms
through the years, the paint was still fresh and bright.

The houses were constructed from half-hewn logs
placed vertically, the roof being thatched and rounded
in the shape of a bell. The houses had one low door in
the front, with a high window in the back probably
doing duty as a chimney. Few Russians were left, but in
these same houses the natives ate and slept and smoked
their fish. All along the sandy beach the fish could be
seen hanging on the racks.

Loaded with wood and having again exchanged
freight for freight, the sandy shore line was left behind
and they traveled northward again. More small cabins

and clusters of cabins flashed by, summer fishing camps and winter trapping cabins. Thence onwards came villages with such Eskimo names as Ikogmut, Cako, Dog Fish Village, and Pimute.

Captain Healy promised they would arrive at Holy Cross early in the evening. During the entire afternoon Father Crimont strained his eyes to get the first possible glimpse of the mission. He knew only that it was on the left bank and he watched mile after mile of cottonwood and willow trees, with a few spruce, and yet the mission did not appear. After Pimute, he had seen only two small fishing camps. The wooden frames which had supported drying fish, and the ashes from recent camp fires, told of late summer fishing activity.

He had the greatest admiration for this Captain who could maneuver the boat without hitting snags or shoals or sand bars, when to the untrained eye the water's surface looked always the same. Numerous great branches called sloughs floated off from the Yukon. Green-carpeted islands lay in the channel, and low hills could be seen flanking it. The river valley at some points looked very wide and complex.

When evening came and they had not yet arrived Father Crimont wondered whether the Captain had by mistake followed one of the sloughs instead of the main stream of the Yukon. As the young priest stood at the prow of the boat scanning the shore, no one suspected him of these misgivings. The doubts had to do only with the arrival of the boat, not with himself, for already he loved the country. And already he loved its people—his

fellow missionaries, the Eskimo, the Indians, the Miners
—they'd all be his people before long. He had come to
teach them the way to happiness, to Heaven, and how to
save their souls while attending to their daily chores.
He foresaw no difficulties. It had taken him only a short
time to make himself understood among the Crows, so
that now he did not dread the learning of the new native
dialects. And he didn't expect to have as much trouble
with the new language as he had had with English
when he first came to Woodstock eight years before, and
when Father John Wynne and other friends devoted
their free hours to coaching him.

He already loved Alaska—the great wilderness of it,
the vastness, the blue, blue skies with their billowy
clouds, the purple fireweed so plentiful along the shores,
the great areas of berry bushes, even the willow trees,
though they were evidence enough of the poor soil. For
besides that and the cottonwood and the scanty spruce,
very few other species would grow. The river was
muddy too, and not even on a crystal-clear day would
it reflect a blue sky. But the great open expanse appealed
to him. He felt he could stop at any point along the
shore, erect a flagpole, and declare it God's country.

But suddenly his keen eyes penetrated the distance to
the dim outline of the left bank: the line of trees was
broken, and beyond the green, little humps of brown
and white stood out against the softly sloping hillside.

"There it is," Captain Healy called from the Pilot's
house.

The August sun was riding just below the tree-lined

hills in back of the mission. Soon the whole community hove into sight growing larger and larger in the process. First came the tiny settlement consisting of the native village, then further back nearer the sloping hill were the small chapel and other buildings, and—what was still hidden from view—a small garden trying in the long days to reach its growth before the early frost of middle September.

The boat was expected, and long before it reached the landing, a swarm of Eskimo and Indian boys had gathered. In their midst, wearing a cap, was Father Francis Monroe, with whom Father Crimont had gone through school in France, and who had preceded him to Alaska by only one year. They were a long distance from home. After a hearty welcome, he looked beyond his friend toward the boat, and the new missionary knew what was in his mind. "I am alone," he said.

The Sisters were rushing down the path to greet him and the children were singing a welcome song.

"I have come to stay," he cried. And his promise lasted longer than he dreamed.

The boat had stopped chugging, but the angry barking of the sled dogs tied along the river bank continued.

VIII
Life at Holy Cross
[1894-1901]

THE MOST peaceful time I have ever known was my visit to Holy Cross on the Yukon. Our plane circled over the mission one June night at 10:30 and it was still so light that I took a picture from the air which came out clearly. Though it was after bed time, a dozen native boys quickly gathered on the airfield, and with them was Father Spils to welcome us.

There is not a great deal of change between the mission life that Father Crimont first came to, and that which goes on today. The spirit of light-hearted poverty which so filled the air must have come right down from his time. At great effort a garden spot was wrestled out of the wilderness.

A T HOLY CROSS generous extremes were the order of the day. The community was extremely happy. And yet its poverty was a thing to be wondered at. We are told that young Father Crimont was the soul of the family: he was Spiritual Director, and his words "were like sparks from the Heart of Our Lord." He excelled them all in attracting souls to God, and he worked to promote devotion to the Sacred Heart, and to encourage frequent Communion. Each day he taught Christian doctrine, and made the classes so interesting no one wanted to miss them. Whenever any little feast occurred he would say a few words before Mass.

His devotion took an extremely practical form. For instance, we have a leaflet in his handwriting called the Spiritual Treasury done on a duplicator for each child and teacher in the community. The headings are Rosary, Communion, self denial, masses, penance, hours of work, conquests of pride, acts of kindness, good example, etc., and below is a space for each day of the month. With the scarcity of pencils, the children punched holes with pins in each square to keep their personal record of achievement. On each first Friday, the leaflet was handed in as an offering to the Sacred Heart.

Every notable feast was ushered in with a novena. Nightly during the month of June, when work was over

at six o'clock, there was a sermon and Benediction and
Father Crimont took special care in organizing a beautiful service for the first Friday of the month. After the
mass the celebrant read an inspired act of reparation
in which the congregation made the answers. At Christmas the Sisters gave Father Crimont notebooks in which
to write meditation themes for them; and the notes took
some such form as follows: "Let me come to You, Oh
Lord, by the way You wish. It will always then be the
way I wish"; and "Our Lord is a continual Communion to those who do His will."

It is said that in his sermons he made everything
vivid. He would point to the picture of Our Lady and
St. Joseph on their way to Bethlehem. Then he would
say how all could accompany them on the way by
practicing patience, kindness, and faith. He used to sit in
the confessional for hours and his sympathetic under-
standing of problems lifted the children up. He used to
say: "Keep your eyes on Our Lord, and your defects
will fall just like the leaves in autumn."

Father Crimont is said to have been responsible for
the beautiful order in which the ceremonies were carried out at Holy Cross. He wrote out in long-hand a
minute description of the ceremonies to be held during
the liturgical year. Ever since, the manner of procedure
has been scrupulously followed. Sister Mary Winifred
said of that time: "His teaching was Christlike, and it
stayed with you. He made Our Lord a living person,
made you feel familiar with Him, and gave you a
knowledge and love of Our Lord that you couldn't find

anywhere. I never recall any of those feast days without having his words ringing in my ears."

Of course the vestments in those days were poor too. There were no vases, the luxuriant wild flowers sitting in shining catsup bottles. The immaculate altar cloths were starched proud and stiff as the most elegant linen.

The Gospel was preached not only to the children in the school, but to the townspeople as well. When the Koserefsky Indians had seen the opposite bank of the Yukon teeming with life, they obtained permission to build houses on the mission ground. And so a regular Indian village sprang up near the school. Though at this time the post office address was still Koserefsky, the community was known as Holy Cross. It was those same Indians who a few years before had gone to Anvik to ask Father Robaut to settle among them. But even after this personal invitation, the natives were not eager to be converted to Catholicism, and did nothing beyond occasionally attending church. They belonged to the Russian church whose priest came once a year to baptize the children and to give communion to all, leaving them meanwhile without school or regular teaching, and never interfering with their superstitions. Hence, when the Indians realized what the Catholic priest would demand of them, their fervor cooled.

Over and above the routine work, there were the long treks over the tundra and over the river ice by dogsled or on snowshoes to give the last sacraments to a dying native, or to visit the mission stations. This involved the mastery of an art wholly new to the missionaries. The

evening before long trips, the sled was brought into the
cabin to be loaded. It was light in weight, being nine
feet long and 18 inches wide, resting low on the ground
with a cross-bar at the end to guide it. The framework
was laced together with thongs of sealskin, no nails or
screws being used. The load consisted of the teakettle,
frying pan, a few dishes, a handful of dry chips, a bag
of tea, sack of flour, small bag of sugar, and a large
quantity of fish; also valises, the portable altar, and
rolls of blankets convertible into cushion seats. The over-
lapping borders of the large canvas sheet which had
first been spread over the floor of the sled was next
folded over the top, and tucked well in. The whole was
bound with a small rope. With nine or more voracious
dogs consuming a good-sized fish a day, the problem of
carrying along enough dog food was a big one, and
frequently more fish would have to be bought for them
from villages along the way. Since the dogs were always
hungry, they were not averse to gnawing the skin ropes
which held together the frame of the sled.

These long treks by sled meant great hardship to the
newer men, for the bitter cold was only slowly gotten
used to. The large hood of the parka sheltered the face
and protected it somewhat from the sharp wind and
stinging snow, but the eyebrows and lashes became
enmeshed with icicles, and the breath congealed in
flakes which clung around the edge of the hood and
sometimes cemented it to the face. The dogs, no matter
what veterans they were, had a hard time of it as well.
Often, the varying temperatures caused a number of

layers of ice crusts to form, and as the dogs' feet crunched into the crust, they became very sore and often bled. When conditions were especially bad, the dogs would be fitted with shoes, but these soon wore through and sometimes slipped off.

In the early period, the inspiring picture of spiritual vigor and profound happiness at the mission was like a flaming light in a dark cave. For the lack of conveniences, the lack of proper food, the bitterness of the winters, the absence of communication with the outer world—all these things could under ordinary conditions have been a heavy burden. Actually the hardship was lightened by love of God and this spiritual warmth melted all the rigors of the winter.

In those days they had to make cakes without eggs, because eggs could not be kept from freezing. Then as now, they had no chickens, for it is necessary to import baby chicks from the outside each year if the breed is to be kept healthy. The lack of grown vegetables and fruit was also a tremendous handicap. As a result, some of the missionaries, in their very first years, developed scurvy, some being affected only slightly and others in the extreme. When the disease was bad, the patient was not only covered with open sores, but the gums would be affected so that they would recede and the teeth would drop out. It is interesting to know that as a cure they grated raw potatoes, and added a small amount of vinegar for flavoring. The grater was a piece of tin rolled out flat, then punctured at regular intervals with a nail. This sad situation had not been bad among the white people after the first few winters, for they soon found green leaves which they made into salad, and got their minerals from dried berries which in the summer could be gathered in great quantities.

Their food consisted generally of salt corn beef, salt pork, butter, and dried fruits, which they received by the barrel. Dried prunes were always on the table, and these as well as dried apples they ate after long soaking in water. Each year they extended the garden, and at great effort raised their own vegetables. But all the staple food had to come via Seattle and up the river from St. Michael, and the annual shipment was the occasion of some strange happenings. Once through a mistake Holy Cross was sent a double shipment of sugar and no salt, the reverse happening in Akulurak. But on discovering the mistake, there was no consternation. The Sisters merely laughed. "Next year we will have it," they said. It seems they made use of salt brine and got along very well, but Akulurak found it more awkward to do without sugar for the whole year.

Sardine tins were used as soap dishes. The wooden tubs had to keep soaking all the time otherwise they would dry and crack and could not be used when wash day came. It was so cold they sometimes threw buckets of water all over the outside of the house in order to obtain an ice covering to keep the wind out. Otherwise there was only moss and rags between the chinks of logs. The job of inserting these was a seasonal occupation in the fall, and was followed each spring by their removal. But not in the way you would expect. The cows when let out of the barn in the spring were always ravenous, and coming to the house would chew the moss and rags right out from between the logs.

Though freight from the outside world was so expensive and took so long, the Arctic was kind in the way of wild food. In spring there were beaver, ducks, geese, lush, pike. In summer, salmon, whitefish and a dozen kinds of berries. In autumn, chickens, grouse, ducks, ptarmigan and lush. In winter, jack rabbits, arctic hare, ptarmigan, and an occasional moose. The food looks luxurious on paper, but not on the table, for fresh meat was exceedingly scarce and without refrigeration in the summer, the food would not last. The summers were only a little cooler than those of Rochester, New York. Though it was not unusual during the salmon run to bring in 1,000 pounds a day, the fish lost some of its flavor when seen on a plate every day through the year. Nor was it unusual to go for three or four months without any fresh meat at all.

Meanwhile these early years were taking their toll. The foundation was to go on continuously, come hardship from weather, pain, poverty, loneliness, or desolation: and of these first thirteen Jesuit fathers, three had already died before the turn of the century.

Father Tosi, having spent thirty-three years on the Indian missions, the last twelve being in Alaska, died as a result of pneumonia followed by temporary paralysis. Next died Father William Judge who had spent ten years in Alaska and who, on the discovery of gold in the Yukon, followed the miners to Dawson, building a church and hospital. Even before the hospital was completed, it was filled beyond capacity, for typhoid fever had swept over the community. Night and day he served the patients, sleeping on a little cot in the corner so that he could help anyone at a moment's notice. Many of the patients had been exhausted beyond their strength by the march over the Chilkoot trail and had arrived at Dawson in a dying condition. In the mid-winter of 1899, although stricken with incipient pneumonia himself, he answered a sick-call in town, then came home to the hospital and died.

One of the men said of him. "I always felt when I talked with Father Judge as if I were with one who was goodness itself. He left with me the feeling that I wanted to go off by myself and pray. He rarely smiled, but his face was radiant, with an indescribable light."

The third loss was that of Father Muset, who wore himself out in Alaska after only a few years and who came down to the States to die. It was like a battle that went on through the days and through the years while men fell in the fight.

A picture of these early times would be far from complete if one described only the spiritual work, the limitations in food, the physical hardships. The approach of winter brought a new and strange beauty over the land, a play of light and color over the starlit stage. There were the Northern Lights, the sun dogs, the moon dogs, the long sunrises and sunsets in midwinter, the great Yukon river bed blanketed in purest white snow. Then there were the mirages. When the temperature was well below zero, and the day clear, those at Holy Cross could see a phantom ridge of mountains some 30 to 60 miles away. Especially in the mornings as it was getting light, they watched peaks, some symmetrical, others in fantastic shape with jutting pinnacles, or with crests that seemed to hang over the sides like the surge of the sea. The shapes slowly and continually changed their design, sometimes appearing sharp as the Matterhorn, at other times as flat as a plateau. These shady illusions seemed only too real; however, they were but a refracted image of the true mountains.

When the nights were clear and cold, the brilliant stars seemed very close, and once especially the Northern Lights gave a special performance. The rising moon in a cold black sky threw out strikingly strong rays, in four directions—above, below, and on each side, forming a huge cross in the air. At the sides, beams of light projected vertical rays ribbed with the colors of the rainbow. Those beams stretching for miles across the air were called "moon-dogs" by the natives.

IX

Father Lucchesi and the Epidemic

[*1898-1937*]

WHILE AT Holy Cross I talked with Mary Elizabeth Dementieff who lives in the village near the Mission. She is now around seventy years old, of Russian and Eskimo heritage, and remembers vividly the work of the early Fathers at Holy Cross. She has a cultured grace and charm, and her English is exceedingly pleasing with a touch of Russian accent. She and her sister-in-law, Tatiana, figure in the story of the epidemic to be told in the coming chapter.

Her husband, Ivan, has done carpentering as well as running the fish camp for the Mission since 1900. Through the winter his crippled-up form can be seen each morning at mass; but the summer sun (and raw rhubarb, he says) drives the rheumatism from his bones, and he handles the boats and fish nets like a boy.

I F YOU ARE ever fortunate enough to find yourself at
Holy Cross on the Yukon, make your way between
the school and church, past the rectory and up over
the sloping potato field. On the hill beyond you will see
a few white, weather-beaten wooden crosses in the
midst of tall grass. A heavy rope fastening the four
wooden corner posts marks off these special graves. A
strange feeling takes hold of you and a still stranger one
when you read the simple inscriptions of the four Jesuit
fathers and three Jesuit brothers who are buried there.
The feeling is too deep and moving to be conveyed in
mere prose. The cross in the top row at the right reads:

Fr. J. L. Lucchesi, S.J.

b. October 19, 1858   *d.* November 29, 1937

The life lived between these dates was a spectacular
one, and heroic. John Luke Lucchesi was born in
Genoa, Italy, just eight months after Joseph Crimont. He
was first a secular priest and superior of the Seminary
in Genoa, Italy. At the age of 33, he entered the Jesuit
Novitiate at Chieri, Italy. At this time, and until 1907,
the Missions of the Rocky Mountain region and Alaska
were in charge of the Jesuit Province of Turin in Italy.
In 1897 that Province sent Father Lucchesi to America.
He studied for a year at Frederick, Maryland, and the
following September arrived at Holy Cross Mission on

the Yukon, a tall, slim figure, with a short beard which he always wore. He died in his 80th year, having devoted just half his life to the Alaskan natives. During that time he spent eighteen years at Holy Cross, eleven at St. Michael, four on the Yukon Delta, two at Mountain Village near the Bering Sea, and one each at Hooper Bay, Pilgrim Springs, Nulato, and Pimute. All of these places are Eskimo and Indian missions, with practically no white people. When he reached Holy Cross in 1898, Father Lucchesi began to study the Eskimo language, and it was not long before he was using it in the confessional.

In the summer of his third year there took place one of the tragedies which happens only a few times in a century. A mysterious plague swept down the coast from Nome, spreading like fire to every village along the lower Yukon and Kuskokwim regions, killing off entire villages. Some believe that the germ originated on the shores of Siberia, and came over with the reindeer brought to Alaska. No such disaster had been known since smallpox in 1837. Opinion was divided as to its identity. Some called it cholera, some influenza, others typhoid. Others again diagnosed it as grippe followed by measles. There was no question as to its deadliness. Before the advent of whaling and fishing boats, there were no plague germs in the country, and consequently no epidemics. The natives had built up no immunity to such diseases, and so when this epidemic came, after destroying whole families and entire villages, its germs stealthily accompanied the cargo on river boats to the next village. Two years earlier, in 1898, Holy Cross Mission counted 195 steamers passing on their way to the gold fields near Dawson. The year of the epidemic, though the number of boats had decreased, enough were yet passing to pick up and deposit the germ with rapidity.

In the early summer Father Lucchesi took a small group of older boys and girls to get the salmon catch. They rowed down the Yukon and into one of the sloughs which had been formed by the floods. From their fishing camp they could see tents dotting both banks of the river some distance away. Father Lucchesi rowed with a few of the children down to the camp. Here he found a great many of the natives sick and others already dead. Father gave them medicine, but on each visit he found more dead people in the tents. The daily toll of the plague was so rapid that little could be done to save their lives. So he devoted all his energies toward saving their souls. He took Mary Elizabeth and Tatiana Dementieff, who knew the dialect of that village, and through them reached every individual, teaching them all the truths necessary for their Baptism. Many he prepared for death.

The natives would not bury their dead for fear of catching the disease, so the missionary and a few of the mission children wrapped the bodies in skins, in the bark of trees, or in their deer-skin bedding. Grass mats coffined them. As there were too many bodies to dig graves for, they transported them some distance by canoe and left them among the brush. One morning, after a month of this activity, they arrived to find on one side of the slough only one woman and two small children yet alive: on the other side only one man.

The task had gotten beyond the workers. After sending these few survivors to another village, Father Lucchesi lowered the tents over the remaining dead bodies and returned to Holy Cross. There he found another battleground. Again only the natives were stricken. There were forty bunks for girls in double tiers around the edge of the dormitory, with a double row in the center. If a girl died during the night a sheet was spread over her bed until morning. There was never a death agony: they fell asleep like babies. And the next morning, those who awoke could see what had happened.

The villagers were also desperately ill. Two priests and one brother were all that remained to dig the graves and make the coffins. Since lumber was scarce they tore up an old boat for this purpose, but after the first few days they dug one large grave, rolled up the bodies in blankets, and placed them side by side without coffins.

Sister Mary Winifred, who took care of the patients, said they had no fear of death, and were more like children eager to get home for the holidays. When a child noticed a companion nearing the end, the stronger one would slip out of bed, come to the dying one and say, "You come for me next." One child, who was sinking fast, told Sister that a beautiful lady had come to see her, and said she would come for her soon.

Forty-one years later, and only a half year before she died, Sister Winifred told edifying stories which show the throbbing faith and burning devotion of those Holy Cross children. The epidemic had been raging through a good part of the summer and showed no signs of surcease. During the novena in preparation for the first Friday of August, Father Crimont, discouraged to see so many dying, made promises to the Sacred Heart, asking that the epidemic be stopped. It was a pact made between God and the whole community. Nearing midnight on the eve of the first Friday, an Indian girl named Louise commenced to die. Father Crimont knelt on one side of the bed, and Sister Winifred on the other. Sister whispered to Louise that soon it would be the first Friday, and the three began offering together, "O Jesus, through the Immaculate Heart of Mary, etc." When they reached the part of the prayer for the particular request, Sister suggested "to obtain my cure." But Louise protested in a voice choked with tears. "No, Sister, please, I am so near heaven I want to go." While they prayed one of the other children came over to the bed and asked Louise to come for her next. But she answered in a loud voice: "I'll come for nobody."

She died that night; the epidemic stopped, and there were no more deaths that year.

Such a story seems more like a page out of a fable than a true account of happenings in our lifetime. But the missions abound in stories having more than an ordinary flavor of the supernatural. Thus, then ended

the epidemic of 1900 at Holy Cross. But the story of
Father Lucchesi and his work at the Indian village is
not finished. The following spring there was another
fishing expedition, and he again took the native children
with him to get the year's supply of salmon. They
pitched their tents in the same place where they had
been the preceding year. Then Father forbade anyone
of the fishing crew to visit the now deserted village
further down the slough. But that first night he left the
camp, rowed down to the village of death, lifted the
tents and saw beneath them the revolting sight of de-
composing flesh and bones of the plague-stricken victims. He blessed the bones and the flesh that clung to
them, and buried the remains. The odor must have been
insupportable. Certainly, from the purely human viewpoint such a task voluntarily embraced can hardly be
understood.

The month of May was almost gone, and except for
a short time at midnight, the sun shone steadily. Each
night the priest left the fishing camp; and each morning before the young fishers were awake, he would
return quietly, removing first the cassock which covered
him on these nightly trips. Already it had taken on a
suffocating odor.

When the dead were buried, he gave his garment to
Mary Elizabeth and Tatiana Dementieff, asking them
to wash it. But he charged them—"tell no one of this."
Not until many years after was the story known. But
today, almost a half century has passed, and people still
speak of it, and of the young priest who gave himself

without measure. His whole forty years in the Arctic spelled a life of heroic mortification.

Once an Italian Cardinal, a relative of his, wrote begging him to return to Italy where his talents could be used for the greater benefit of the Church. Father Lucchesi replied, "The talents I have, God gave me to save my soul, and it is here in Alaska I can save it."

It is said that he was a genius in self-sacrifice. He was always considerate of others and doing acts of kindness for them. But for himself, he allowed no comforts, sleeping only four hours at night and that, on boards. Once, when he stayed overnight at the home of a trader, he was furnished with a soft bed. The next morning the trader to his astonishment found him on the floor. The missionary remonstrated he wasn't used to a soft bed. He rose every morning at four, said mass at 5:15, then sat at his Corona typewriter to take care of his mail.

He was a puzzle to the most hardened of the other white mushers. He raced on his journeys, stopping only for brief periods of rest. Once he kept up a continuous trip for six days. At times in the blinding blizzard when it was impossible for the dogs to go on, he would dig into the snow. He was always buoyant, and during these trips would cry out repeatedly: "See how God in his Providence provides tenderly for these souls."

One of the stories told of him gives an idea of the constant threat of pain and hazard that hovered always near by. One of the early winters found him on the trail bringing a young boy for the school. The river ice had grown thin from constant wearing of a sand whirl underneath. The ice suddenly gave way, the dogsled, dogs, missionary, and pupil were thrown into the swift icy waters.

The husky dogs climbed out of the river, shook the water from their fur, and with nothing to hold them back, raced for home with the sled behind them.

The two mushers found it more difficult. They reached their arms out and grappled for a spread of solid ice. Despite the swift waters which pulled their heavy clothing ever back and down, they finally gained the river bank. Almost immediately each was encased in solid ice, for the temperature was 50 below zero. They hammered off the icy case from each other, but in the darkness could find nothing with which to make a fire: their plight was still extremely dangerous. The only thing left was to stamp and dance until morning when they found part of a dry log, and, on returning to the spot of the near-tragedy, discovered a waterproof match case. Happily they made a fire, had a cup of tea, and started on their way. These hardships strengthened his endurance, as every day he guided his life rigorously by spiritual principles.

Perhaps the best picture we can give of Father Lucchesi is the one he drew in honor of his countryman and fellow priest, Anthony Keyes, who died in 1928.

"Father Keyes had renounced a splendid career in Italy as a preacher, as he had a natural gift of eloquence, perfected by his intense spiritual life and love of study; instead of churches crowded with admiring listeners, he found a wilderness of ice and snow, with

Church, School and Convent at Holy Cross.

(Photo by Father Hubbard)

Holy Cross on the Yukon.

Father Monroe and Father Crimont.

Father Tom Cunningham of Little
Diomede Island near Siberia.

Father Menager.

few Eskimo, scattered over an immense area into innumerable and ever-changing hamlets. Not for a moment did he ever feel the least regret for the sacrifice
he made. For 28 years he worked continually and
heroically, seeking them in their underground hovels,
teaching them there, plodding for hours in the snow, in
bitter cold weather, in the storms, in the blizzards. His
zeal, his earnestness was irresistible, and he converted
hundreds and founded several missions for them. At 62,
already worn out by his generous zeal, he contracted
the illness that brought his life to an end. Gifted with a
cheerful disposition and optimism, he was charitable,
obliging and warmed all the hearts that approached
him by his simple piety and lively faith. As was his life,
so was his end: he died as the saints die."

Collecting all that we can find from friends who speak
of Father Lucchesi and those who wrote of him, we
can only feel that these words, written in admiration of
another, paint a true picture of himself.

Father Keyes' name was originally Chiavassi, but
since its pronunciation was difficult for the natives, he
shortened it. He was simple to the end of his days.
Three years before his death, this same man of great
learning, wrote from Mountain Village, "I am a poor
Dago some 25 years talking Eskimo. What barbarous
English can you expect from me. I have been eight
years living alone with the Eskimo!"

He died as he had lived, like a saint.

Early in 1937 the doctor advised Father Lucchesi to
do no more stair-climbing, to take light walks only, to

have a moderately simple diet, with lots of rest and an afternoon nap. He recommended a bromide or some sleeping tablets if he grew restless. And he advised him to keep an adequate supply of tincture of digitalis on hand.

As this, his eightieth year, wore on, he suffered severe attacks of asthma, and was forced to sit in a straight chair both day and night. No complaint ever dropped from his lips. He had an encouraging word for the least little native. The village people looked on him as a saint, and had the greatest confidence in his prayers and blessing. Toward the end, the village women vied with each other to relieve the Sisters who took care of him. He said Mass up to the last two weeks before he passed away.

The day they laid him to rest on the hill at Holy Cross, a heavy snowfall had turned the countryside white.

X

The Alaskan Hercules, Father Monroe

[1893-1940]

I ARRIVED in Alaska just seven months after Father Monroe's death, and in both Wrangel and Juneau I heard people still talking of him in hushed tones. Later throughout the interior of Alaska I felt his profound influence. Next to Bishop Crimont, his stay there was longest—forty seven years.

The breath-taking sacrifice of which we shall hear—it began in 1933 and ended only with his death seven years later—was told me by Bishop Crimont. Mr. Edwin Edgerly later showed me a letter from His Excellency written in 1933 which quoted Father Monroe's letter, simple and straightforward in its understatement, but epic when taken with the events which followed.

I T WOULD BE HARD to find a record of association to
rival in length that of Francis Monroe and Joseph
Crimont. They first met at La Providence College
in Amiens in 1873. Then in the Novitiate at St. Acheul
Francis was Sacristan and Joseph, his assistant, and
junior by two years, learned from him the intricacies of
church decoration. Often they could be seen, brushes
attached to their feet, pushing along on the chapel floor,
waxing and polishing the hard wood. They were together again at St. Helier, and for most of their work
in France and Belgium. In 1886 the two Jesuits came to
America with Paul Muset.

Francis Monroe was born in the Chateau of Perreux,
not far from Lyons, France, in 1855. At the Jesuit College of Metz, Lorraine, he was a classmate of Marshal
Foch. Arriving in America, he spent one year at Woodstock, Maryland, during which he underwent several
severe operations. The following summer he was appointed Minister at Gonzaga College in Spokane; later
he spent four years at St. Peter's Mission at Fort Benton,
Montana; then he was again sent to Spokane. Next
he became missionary to the Crow Indians, traveling on
horseback from camp to camp; and though we have
no writings of this period to substantiate our surmise,
we can read between the lines the beginning of great
physical hardships. For one with no first-hand knowledge of primitive conditions and with a physical endur-

ance as yet untried, the adjustment must have been severe. We can picture this bright, energetic, young missionary bouncing off his horse, being welcomed by the Indians emerging from their tents. His cheeks were round like shining apples and he had bright blue eyes. In traveling from one Indian camp to another, he took no supplies with him, but ate with the people wherever he happened to find himself at meal time. Accustomed to French cooking, the Indians' food must have been a perpetual shock to him.

Father Monroe left enlightening accounts of the beginnings of Eagle, Alaska. Needless to say his records are severely objective, including no word of his own weariness, his own suffering. We can imagine, however, all the danger and difficulties that crowded into this summer trip of 1895.

By that time he had lived at Holy Cross for one year and at Nulato for another year. His third summer in Alaska he was asked to make a preliminary excursion, alone and on foot, into a country full of bears, where roads and even trails were yet unknown. His destination was Eagle, located at Mission Creek some twelve miles below the point where the Yukon River crosses the Canadian-Alaskan boundary line. Two years later several thousand people had gathered at the place, and after another four years he returned to begin a permanent mission there. But on this his first trip, only scattered tents along the creeks dotted the wilderness.

On July 2, 1895, he reached Miller Creek some sixty miles from Forty Mile Post, and there baptized Joseph

Hubert and Bernard Albert Day, twins, the first white children born in this part of the Yukon Territory. A few days afterwards he climbed the high divide at the head of the creek with a miner named McDonald, who was going to Forty Mile Post for his yearly supplies. The freight was ordinarily packed to the creeks by horses, at 25 cents a pound, but this cost was prohibitive to McDonald, who could be seen bent under his load plodding the thirty miles between the river and his diggings. He made the trip again and again until the supplies had all been transported to his camp.

From the trail on the summit he pointed out the direction Father Monroe was to take, remarking that it would be a long time before he met another priest. So he gave the missionary three dollars asking him to say masses for his departed relatives. This largesse left McDonald with less than a dollar in his pocket, but that too he gave. Fortunes were made fast in those days. Only a few years later Alexander McDonald had earned the title of Klondike King, and he presented Father Judge, who had worked among the miners at Dawson, with a check for $30,000 to pay the bills of the hospital.

Following the direction pointed out by McDonald, Father Monroe reached the first mining settlement of the trip ; it was called The Little Ireland, named for its men. They did not know the country, but the next morning after mass, they gave the missionary six and one-half ounces of gold dust and directed him to Davis Creek where Davis, a hunter, trapper, and miner, could direct him.

On reaching the creek Mr. Davis took the priest to a summit and pointed out a high range of mountains with two white peaks.

"Keep these two high points always before you; after [so many] miles you will come to a low summit from where you will see in a distance the valley of Forty Mile; and on the other side several creeks running into the Forty Mile. Look for one with two lines of white spots: that is Franklin Gulch; the white spots are the tents of the miners. It is the only creek inhabited in the country. Now turn left, and look for a sharp divide. Follow it, and count all the creeks running from there into the Forty Mile River at your right; the fifth will be Napoleon Creek where you are going."

The directions seemed simple to Father Monroe, and all through the night he made his way through scraggy brush, and over rough, hilly ground. Fortunately this far north little darkness dims Alaska's July skies. When the early morning dew fell on the land, he came far above Jack Wade Creek where the valley was deep. Having crossed it he climbed an elevation of six or seven hundred feet to the other side. He felt tired and hungry, so he rested, then he hurried down the hill amid the thorny bushes and rocks, and climbed the next one. But at this point he had lost his bearings. He had to retrace his steps, and return to the place where he had rested. From there he again saw the two white peaks, on which he had unknowingly turned his back.

The second attempt was successful. He reached the opposite summit, found the peaks where they should be, and walked toward them until late in the afternoon. Then he came to the small eminence from which he could see the tents of the miners nestled seven or eight miles ahead in the Gulch. He turned to the left, recognized the sharp divide, and counted the creeks running from its summit. At the fifth he descended toward Forty Mile River, some three miles away. Most of the traveling meant breaking way through brush and climbing formidable hills, for there were neither trails nor roads. No soul was to be seen, nor house either. He walked back to the divide, but then did not know what to do. He could not decide whether Napoleon Creek was further on, or if it was the one he had just passed. Though the divide was rising higher and higher, he resolved to go ahead. Still, there was no sign of his creek.

It was getting late and he had nothing to eat. At last he came to a deep valley with a fine downward slope. There he found an empty cabin. Soon he found another, and another, but all were abandoned. At length he came to a newly dug ditch, and standing alongside was a brand new shovel! He wanted to shout for joy. He followed the ditch and presently came up behind a man and woman salting moose meat the door of their cache.

From this point Father Monroe visited all the miners at Franklin Gulch, and two days later with a party of prospectors and trappers, he almost drowned when his boat swamped in treacherous Forty Mile River. He next floated down the Yukon some 225 miles to the new and booming Circle City, for gold had been discovered on Birch Creek nearby.

Again he visited every stream where mining was carried on. This was also a trackless waste, and each man wading through swamps infested with mosquitoes, was confident he had struck the shortest way from Circle to the creeks.

On this tramp, the Indian water boots the priest was wearing became too dry and brittle, so he took them off and with stones to weight them down, put them into the creek: then he went to rest. Soon he heard the snarling of quarreling dogs, and on trying to separate them found that his boots were the object of their fight. He had nothing with which to replace his unrecognizable footgear except a pair of light moccasins, and these soon wore out in plodding over the rocks. Everywhere miners offered him their shoes, but they were all too large and heavy. The rest of his 500-mile trip, through the uncharted wilderness, Father Monroe leaves to our imagination.

He resumed the story four years later in August of 1899 when he was sent to Eagle to take charge. There he bought for $300.00 a site which contained two log cabins, and not long after added seven more lots. These he made into a garden, the produce of which was the only means of keeping him alive.

This mining camp was only a few years old, and the miners, even if they were so inclined, had had no opportunity of attending mass. When Father Monroe arrived as resident priest, the fifty Catholics in and around the town were for a long time too busy with their search for gold to return to church. So it was that in the first year there was practically no activity at the church: no baptisms, no marriages, no burials. This was indeed a depressing condition for a zealous young priest who had come 6,000 miles to preach the Gospel. But we find no gloomy reaction in his account.

Ordinary labor was 75 cents or $1.00 an hour, and Father Monroe, unable to afford the luxury of a helper, was his own housekeeper, carpenter, and gardener. He did not have enough spiritual work to keep him busy, so he went around trying to help people who were poor and sick. Living alone in a miserable shanty in the fall of 1900 he found an old man in a dying condition. Since civilians could not be admitted to the military hospital, Father Monroe brought the man to one of the Mission cabins, nursed him, prepared him for death, and buried him. As others became ill the people realized that something had to be done for the needy sick, and requested Father Monroe to start a small hospital. In an hour, $750.00 was subscribed for its beginning. The good work continued for three years until the fall of 1903, when civilians were accepted at the military hospital. During these years patients were brought from hundreds of miles around, and for several years Father Monroe maintained the hospital. Each spring he visited on foot the miners all over the country from Eagle and Forty Mile, up to Dawson, and the money they gave him made the hospital possible. In the winter of 1902–1903 gold was discovered in the Tanana Valley, and in 1904 the town of Fairbanks sprang up. Here Father Monroe remained for twenty years.

Another tale about Father Monroe is still being talked about in Alaska today. The first Catholic church in Fairbanks was built in the middle of the town, while the hospital stood some distance across the river. As the work of both institutions grew, and there was more and more call on the priest's time, it became urgent that the church and hospital should be side by side. Father Monroe decided that it was possible to move the church through the town and across the river to the hospital site. He was alone in his optimism, for the townspeople thought the plan impracticable. The nights had turned cold, and the river froze solidly enough to bear the weight of the church. Now the difficult part of the undertaking was the crossing of the river which had to be done diagonally, a distance of some 400 feet. Father Monroe conceived an ingenious plan: two lines were drawn on the ice thirty feet apart and holes in the ice were cut at every eight feet along these lines. In these holes strong junks of logs were wedged and left to freeze. On the following day, all the tops were sawed two inches above the ice, making the strongest and cheapest support for the heavy timber on which the church was rolled.

The next and last challenge was the steep 25-foot elevation from the river level to the new structure. During this whole work Father Monroe carried the responsibility, and at this point he insisted on having a second cable added to the first. Just when the church was touching the foundation, the old cable broke, and the new one saved the church from rolling full speed

down to the river. Winter was making further work
impossible: but it was resumed the following spring,
and was continued from year to year until 1924 when
Father Monroe was transferred from Fairbanks to
Wrangell, a small town in southern Alaska carved out
of the mountain side.

Feats of carpentry and engineering were not new to
him. In his young days in France he had shown himself
an excellent carpenter. Father Grandidier, the provincial, remarked at the time that had Father Monroe not
become a missionary, he would have made a fine architect, and that he had hoped at one time to put him in
charge of the construction in the province.

During his vacation in Lyons before leaving for America the young priest applied his ingenuity in making a
portable altar, every piece of which fitted compactly
one into the other and served several purposes: the
chalice became a monstrance for Benediction by merely
screwing off the cup. He was also instrumental in building nearly all the churches in the interior of Alaska.

Father Monroe possessed unusual strength and endurance and pluck. Once while at Holy Cross he heard that
a prospector was desperately ill some miles away. He
went to his cabin, found him very sick with scurvy, and
said he must come to Holy Cross to be nursed back to
health. In his refusal to go, the old sour-dough exhausted
his entire Alaskan vocabulary. But the missionary would
not listen; he merely carried him over his back to the
mission where he soon became well again.

After he had been in Wrangell nine years, a serious

accident happened to him. Here is his own account of it:

"We were building a scaffolding ten feet high to support a platform from which we could work on the ceiling of the church. We had completed one trestle, a timber 25 feet long fitted with 3 ten-foot legs, and had set it up against the wall. My helpers were engaged in constructing a similar set while I was taking some measurements. Without warning the heavy trestle started to topple upon us. Thanks to Divine Providence I perceived the danger in time to warn my companions. With upraised arms I broke somewhat the force of the blow, but the timber grazed my cheek and struck me full upon the chest. The injury to my ribs prevented me doing any of the heavier work afterward, but now I am feeling much better and expect to recover completely in a short time. Oddly, my glasses, though thrown across the room, did not get broken; and the blow to my cheek, while painful, did a very neat job of removing a large wart. I was not knocked unconscious, and I am thankful that my injuries are so slight, as compared to what they might have been."

After being forced to keep his bed for a short while, Father Monroe took no more care of his health nor did he refer to it again.

The accident of the falling timber occurred in 1933. His friends noticed that, though already bent, he now stooped, in fact was almost hunchbacked. It was only when he said mass that he seemed by incredible effort able to lessen the right-angled position of his body.

In 1939, about ten months before his death, he had to go to the hospital in Seattle. There, six years after the mishap, it was discovered that his back had been broken! The doctors said that it must have been very painful at the beginning when the timbers fell on him, and that gradually he had become used to it.

Nulato, Alaska.

Father Jette with his natives.

King Islanders rest inside their skin boats.

(Photo by Father Hubbard)

Eskimo fishing for tom cod at Unalakleet.

XI

Father Jette and the Middle Yukon

[1898-1927]

THE STORY of Father Jette's work first took shape for me when his successor Father McElmeel sketched in the lines of his rich personality, his humor, his tireless trips up and down the river. I learned more about him one day in New England, for Father Ambrose Gallagher told of living with him the summer of 1919 when, as a lad just out of school, he went to Alaska looking for gold.

The mission at Nulato is rich in Father Jette's manuscripts. Scientific institutes in Vienna, England and Ireland published his work on the Tena Indians.

ERHAPS NO NATIVE VILLAGE in Alaska has been the subject of more recorded history than Nulato, and we have Father Jette to thank not only for compiling the accounts written by Russian and English historians, but for adding fresh material and viewpoints on the basis of his own investigation.

Besides the voluminous notes in his own handwriting, we have his 25,500 word unpublished manuscript entitled *Jottings of an Alaskan Missionary*. It begins with Bering's discovery of Alaska and takes the history up to 1882 when gold was discovered on the Upper Yukon. His work is a painstaking, meticulous, comparative study of events. In some cases he presented correct versions of local history where original accounts had been garbled and errors perpetuated by indiscriminating historians.

The most interesting case of his critical pen is that of the so-called Nulato massacre of 1851. Before this time the Nulato Indians had already twice destroyed the establishments the Russians had built, and their hostile spirit lived on covered by only a veneer of peace. The warlike Koyukuk natives, who lived twenty-five miles up the Yukon River, decided on an extensive revenge which would involve the Nulato tribe and at the same time annihilate the Russians. The opportunity offered itself in February, 1851, when the Indians were gathered with a related tribe at the post for a potlatch. The

Koyukuks swooped down on their enemies and massacred practically all the natives: they also killed several Russians including Commander Derabin; also Lieutenant John J. Barnard, a British naval officer.

Now Father Jette shows that this affair has been misrepresented in history. Its beginning has to do with the story of the lost Franklin Expedition. In 1850 the Commander of a British ship sent in search of Sir John Franklin's expedition, heard a rumor that the Indians along the Koyukuk River had news of the Franklin party. Since Nulato was the only white settlement near this region, Lieutenant Barnard was sent to spend the winter there, visit the interior, and investigate the rumor.

It was in February of that year that the assault took place. A half mile below the trading post 100 natives were crowded in three large winter-houses, outside of which were their birch-bark canoes. The Koyukuks broke up the canoes, thrust them into the apertures of the roofs and underground crevices, and fired the houses. Those who escaped the flames were shot down outside by arrows.

As described by William H. Dall in *Alaska and Her Resources,* the cause of this massacre was the tactless way in which Lieutenant Barnard summoned the famous Koyukuk chief to come to see him.

But as Father Jette points out, this is obviously incorrect. The real cause was inter-tribal hatred, in addition to a deep hatred of the Russians who had mistreated the natives. The historians coming after Dall accepted his statements regarding the cause of the massacre, and unknowingly perpetuated the untruth.

The Russians had obviously given Dall the wrong information. If the blame could be thrown on the shoulders of the English naval officer, it would be taken away from the Russians at the garrison whose mistreatment of the Indians had incited the retaliation. Father Monroe started this investigation by questioning Indians still alive in 1896 and 1897. It was finished and recorded by Father Jette.

With the massacre of 1851 the Indian tribal warfare seems to have come to a close. But despite this, the natives still lived in constant dread of some fresh attack, and every now and then, even today, someone starts a rumor of a coming invasion.

The next bit of history recorded in Nulato brings to mind today's talk of a railroad across Alaska and Siberia; for in 1860, the Western Union Telegraph Company proposed to connect the old world to the new by running a wire through the two countries, joining them by a short cable across Bering Strait. Robert Kennicott, a young scientific explorer, was in charge of the Alaska end. In 1865, he met William H. Dall and Frederick Whymper, and a few others at St. Michael, and they went to Nulato over the portage from Unalakleet, staying there for the winter.

In 1867, news came of the successful laying of the Atlantic Cable. As a result, the Telegraph Company's northwestern expedition was recalled. Meanwhile Alaska was sold to the United States.

From Ivan Petrof in *Compilation of Narratives of Explorations in Alaska* comes a singularly interesting description of Alaska's reaction to the purchase:

With the roll of drums and the discharge of musketry, the imperial eagle of Russia descended and the Stars and Stripes rose into the murky atmosphere of an Alaskan autumn day. The Princess Maksutof wept at the spectacle, and all nature seemed to keep her company, drenching to the skin all the participants in the ceremony. The native Indians in their canoes, witnessed it from a distance, listening stolidly to the booming of the cannon, and gazing with indifference upon the descending and ascending flags. Of the nature of the proceedings they had a faint and imperfect conception, but one thing they did realize, that the country they once imagined their own was now being transferred to a strange people by what must have appeared to them a singular ceremony.

Another important event in the history of Nulato, which the reader will remember from earlier treatment, was the wintering in 1877 and 1878 of Bishop Seghers where he and Father Mandart studied the language, instructed the natives and baptized the children. The spot where he was murdered eight years later was only one day's journey up the river. From this time on, the history of Nulato is the history of the Catholic Mission there, and many fascinating stories lie buried in the notes of the old missionaries. It was built in 1887–1888 by Father Tosi, with the help of a Canadian named Baudoin.

The work of these early missionaries was hard and challenging, and they had to be men of iron will. The first real challenge came when the Nulato Indians an-

nounced their annual "Feast of the Dead." A portion of
the ground in front of the village was cleared of snow
and enclosed with a fifteen-foot palisade adorned with
pelts, blankets, bows, guns, toboggans, and snowshoes;
in the center of the plot stood a high pole. The six-day
festival consisted of dancing, singing, banqueting, nar-
rating legends of the tribe, and eulogizing the important
people who had died in the course of the year. The cele-
bration, however, included another feature. Two be-
reaved women of the tribe were to appear before the
assembly, and during a frenzied dance, slash their bodies
with knives in token of their grief.

Now it happened that the two widows, who were
chosen to play this role, had been attending Father
Tosi's instructions, and were preparing for baptism.
They consulted him and accepted his advice. When
called upon by the Shamans for the exercises of self-
torture, they boldly refused to step forward, declaring
that decency and Christian principles would not permit
them to partake in such a barbarous ceremony. Little by
little Christian customs were built up in the framework
of the native ideology. Love and kindness took the place
of cruelty. Faith and trust rooted out fear and the un-
certainty of life.

Meanwhile links showing the continuity through the
years shine out like golden beads on a necklace. In the
winter of 1877–1878 a boy named Andrew Antoska was
baptized by Bishop Seghers in Nulato. He was one of
the promising lads whom Father Tosi later taught, and
brought for further instruction to Holy Cross. In the

winter of 1890 and 1891, however, Andrew died, leaving a deep and salutary impression on his people.

Meanwhile Father Judge spent a year at Nulato; also, Father Monroe, who did the ground work for the study of the Indian language. He solved some of the most intricate questions of the grammar, wrote some religious instructions, a Way of the Cross, and a bible history. He recorded legends and historical events told by the old people and a sort of Indian anthology for the use of beginners.

In 1898, Father Julius Jette, S.J., a young priest fresh from the Jesuit Seminary in Montreal and a graduate of the University of Paris, came to Alaska. He was to spend the better part of the next twenty-nine years at various missions along the middle Yukon; at Nulato, then at Tanana, Kokrines, and others. He was thin, of medium height, with very ascetic features. He had a placid expression and seemed undisturbed by emotions of anger and impatience: nothing ruffled him. Not even when the authorities at Fort Gibbon wanted to take away his garden plot for a recreation center. People said that he talked with a delightful Canadian accent, that he was a good listener, and would draw out his companion: he was a perfect host and would give a visitor the feeling that he had all day for him were he Indian or white.

In the summer one could see him in an old linen duster, a small fitted hat, and sometimes if he took the river steamer, he would carry a flowered carpet bag. In those early days he wore a full untrimmed beard and had a few sharp character lines running through his face. His little cabin was filled with books and a big table. A visitor once said he looked like the picture of St. Jerome with a lion on one side, and books piled all over the floor.

During this period he wrote several pioneer books on the Tena (also called Tinnah) language as yet unpublished. One is called "Heavenly Words": 120 pages of prayers, devotions and hymns. But his work in history, in language, and translation took only a part of his life. He was first of all a rugged missionary. Let us relay a description of Father Jette which an old pioneer gave to Father Francis Prange. The man said:

"I've seen him paddle in here in a canoe when it was rainin' cats and dogs, and blowin' out there in the open river like an introduction to the crack of doom. But Father Jette'd come sneakin' along under the shelter of the shore, undisturbed as could be, cuttin' his way thru the storm as tho' he was born to that kind of thing, when everybody knew he was a real scholar and as polished a gentleman as ever breathed. Rough stuff was as foreign to his make-up as a riot in a church, but he took it, as I said, as tho' he was born to it. . . . No sir, I never saw that man tired, tho' I knew that sometimes when he'd come loping along on a pair of snowshoes, he must of snowshoed some 30 miles since his last stop. Yes sir, there wasn't a man within shootin' distance this side of hell that was more welcome right here where you're sittin' now than that little dried-up remnant of a priest that was a man."

Father Jette's frame house in Tanana was on Main Street halfway between the hotel and the entrance of the Fort, and it had a beautiful garden which he had made. People were always wanting to bring him good things to eat, knowing the food he prepared for himself was not tasty: sometimes it consisted of potatoes cooked with their jackets on and boiled dried fish; other times he would cook a quantity of stew and eat of it for three or four days. When people brought him pastry, he would give it to the Indian children.

As he would not be pampered in the way of food, so, too, was he equally adamant when the white people gave him especially warm clothes for winter. He would simply give them away. He had a fur coat, but would never wear it: he wore instead a heavy cloth one.

He used to take the little Indians on his back and swim across the river with them, and he would ride his canoe Indian fashion. In the winter he would put his snowshoes on and tread ahead of the dog team, letting the Indian boy ride. He was constantly going up and down the various rivers visiting Indian settlements. He lived right with the people, and left his impression on everyone with whom he came in contact.

One of his letters written in the early part of the century gives a vivid picture of the work. He tells of his sled being heavily loaded with the customary outfit. He says, "We covered the whole nicely with the two sides of the sled cover, tied it strongly with the last rope so that it would keep into shape even when the sled tipped, finally put the dogs in the harness and after having said the traditional Hail Mary in our beautiful language: Neutra, Mary, ne-tlo raralnith tse rolon, etc., we started half sliding, half tumbling down the beach, reached the main Yukon trail and glided down the river." He also mentioned that the sleeping bag was falling into disuse and becoming old-fashioned. "One gets used to our primitive bed and rests better in this simple arrangement than in the elaborate contrivances of civilized life."

Once when Father Jette went to visit another mission, his dog team driver had been drinking too much and they all fell through the ice. Father Jette walked back to the village with the water solidly frozen about him. People thought he would die, but in a short time he was well again. How many such narrow escapes these missionaries had (and have today, for the conditions today are little different) no one will ever know: their modesty seals tightly any trickle of information about their heroism.

A traveler once asked Father Jette to tell him what hardships he had gone through. He hesitated for a moment as if in thought, then scratched his whiskers as was his habit, and looking his questioner full in the eye acknowledged that yes, he had gone through a few. Then after another brief hesitation, he explained:

"I remember once, in fact a few times, I was given some *very* tough meat to eat!"

It was the late fall of 1924 when he was remodeling into a church and living quarters the hut which the Knights of Columbus had built for the soldiers at Tanana during the first World War. In handling heavy

timbers alone he ruptured himself. It was discovered
he had a very severe case of strangulated hernia. They
brought him by dogsled to Fairbanks, and he almost
died of gangrene on the way. From there he went to
Seattle, and when he was well enough, taught at Seattle
College for a short time. But Alaska beckoned him, and
1927 found him on the boat for Akulurak Mission on
Bering Sea.

But as before he would never spare himself, so now
he would not take the proper care of himself. They
were building a new church at the mission, and as was
usual, were short of help. The brother cook turned
himself into the much needed mason worker, and Father
Jette did the cooking. The water had to be brought
from the river in barrels for daily use. Instead of letting
the boys do the heavy work, Father Jette lifted the
heavy buckets and hurt himself seriously. A few weeks
later he died. When the people heard this, they all
cried, for they loved him very much. He is buried at
Akulurak on the tundra with the high grass blowing
across his grave.

The names of at least two missionaries will go down
in history prominently associated with the fifty-five
years of Nulato's life as a mission center: Father Jette,
who stayed steadily for twenty-six years, and Father
McElmeel, who has been there since 1924.

XII

Shepherd of King Island

[1903]

WHENEVER I read or hear about King Island, I remember the time when a government teacher was needed there, and I almost agreed to take the job, since I had the experience and degree requirements. I really wanted to go, but what could I do with my Sheed and Ward job? Perhaps I didn't have enough of the missionary fortitude to face a bleak Arctic winter.

IF YOU CONSULT an ordinary-sized map of Alaska, you will find King Island only if you know where to look for it. In area and population, it is insignificant. As an illustration of the dignity of human life and the beauty of sacrifice it is an epic.

Your map will show a dotted line running from the Arctic Ocean to the Bering Sea forming an angle at Bering Strait. This is the boundary between the Soviet Union and the United States, or more specifically between Siberia and Alaska. Further south and west of this point lies King Island, ninety miles northwest of Nome, and less than half that distance from its nearest shore line on Seward Peninsula. It is an island of rock, six miles in circumference, rising sheer from the sea, and is inhabited by two hundred cliff-dwelling Eskimo who still bear likeness, both in feature and their perfect craftsmanship, to their Mongolian ancestors.

They live in houses eight feet square and seven feet high. The only entrance in winter is a hole cut out near the floor through which the occupants must wriggle. At night they sleep on bear and walrus skins, which they fold out of sight during the day. Through the winter the men hunt crabs, walrus, seals, whale and numerous kinds of fish. They also carve ivory pieces with great skill. The women gather wild vegetables, mossy grasses and greens, and these they preserve in seal oil and water.

Such is a brief picture of a primitive island untouched by civilization. They lived a good life.

Then came the whaling expeditions, and later the discovery of gold near Nome. Soon the natives began to spend their summers in the mushroom mining camp of Nome where they sold their ivories and furs. They were a prey to colds, and if there was any influenza around, were sure to catch it. The mid-summer nights held no darkness, and the natives roamed the streets attracted by the lights and gaiety. By and by they acquired the taste for starches, sugar and tea. Gradually they began to buy these in exchange for their products, and the new foods became part of their diet. This intake, however, which substituted part of their own nourishing food, served only one purpose. It gratified their palates, but it did not give them the strength needed for their vigorous lives. Strong liquors, which flowed freely in Nome, were an additional temptation.

And so, these unspoiled primitive people made contact with the fringes of civilization. It had nothing to offer them of value in the framework of their own lives, nor did the contact with unscrupulous traders and ships' crews prove anything but harmful. Infant mortality increased, men in but a few generations became noticeably less rugged.

Into their summer world at Nome in 1903 came a short, wiry French Canadian missionary. Gold had been discovered only a few years before, and the town had suddenly grown to 15,000 people. This young priest had just finished his studies at the Jesuit Seminary in Mon-

treal. That was thirty-nine years ago, but it is said that
Bellermine LaFortune still has the head of a boy, the
laugh of a child of six, and a contagious twinkle in his
eyes. His expression is still the same, but from exposure
to sun, wind and pack ice, his skin is tanned and
leathery. The years have knitted his stocky frame into a
powerfully built one. He is quick in movement, speech
and gestures, and there is a gentleness when he greets
the natives with a smile and a rush of Eskimo words.
He meets the white people with the same buoyant
humor in his rapid English with its unmistakable French
accent. He loves his natives. At the same time he is a
hard-headed little realist, and is direct and to the point
in every dealing.

When addressing his flock, he drives home his points
with choppy gestures, talking so rapidly and sincerely,
and gesticulating so convincingly that even though one
might not understand his words, there is no mistaking
his meaning. As he hammers away with Bible stories, or
berates some particular faults, perhaps the most frequent Eskimo word in his vocabulary is "eksinisi" or
"don't you be afraid." This is generously peppered into
his remarks. As he speaks one is conscious of short broad
fingers on a square palm.

When Father LaFortune came to Nome, he could
only be with the natives in the summer, and his efforts
to help them with their problems and teach them religion had at first little results. Only a few received instructions from him; most of them remained Pagans.

At this time the King Islanders had a saintly old

chief named Aresac. In the winter of 1904–05 his daughter became ill and predicted the time on the next day when she would die. Before dying she called her family and friends around her and said:

"God told me that tomorrow I will die. He also told me to tell you to embrace the religion of the Father and be baptized because it is God's Religion."

The following summer when the Eskimo came to Nome they told Father LaFortune the story of the chief's daughter. Gradually the whole tribe took instruction and came into the Church. For many years he taught them each summer at Nome, then he visited the Island and the natives built a chapel overlooking the village.

It was in 1929 that Father LaFortune first accompanied them to King Island for the winter. Since then, except for one year, he has remained with them continuously. He has tried to have them stay on the Island and not go to Nome each year, for its bad effect on them has continued with the years. They became sick from colds—the visits destroyed appreciation for their own lives—they became anxious for baubles. Some would gamble and others would get lazy. He was strict with them too: he wanted the young people to marry their own kind, to work hard and to be honest. He wanted them to build clean, new houses. His efforts were in no way limited to their spiritual needs.

When he settled down to their year-round problems, he saw many practical ways of helping them. For one thing he felt the small increase in population was due

to the excessive work of both men and women. The
men had always dragged the seals they had killed five
miles across the ice, then up a seven hundred foot
northern slope, then across the island, then down the
six hundred feet to the village. Considering that one
seal might weigh two hundred pounds, the energy
expended was tremendous. To solve this problem, he
rigged up a cable and a derrick at the top of the island
by means of which the seals and other game might be
hauled up. Father LaFortune considered this not merely
a method of relieving their back-breaking work, but indeed a device to save the tribe from utter destruction.

Reducing the women's hard work was more difficult.
They would tramp miles over the tundra in search of
sour leaves and roots and wild onions, for the island was
almost barren of vegetation. It was such hard work
gathering these scarce vegetables that it injured their
health and brought them to early graves. To counteract
the condition, the priest transported seeds and planned
to have them grow at least a minimum but regular
supply of their own vegetables. The bad soil and short
growing season needed the addition of a great deal of
optimism. These are but two examples of the missionary's continual efforts to help in their everyday problems. His life had no limitations either of duties or hours.
His was a twenty-four-hour-a-day concern for his flock.

His diary makes fascinating reading. Following is one
entry dated May 26, 1930:

"A deep gloom fell over the village. One of the
strongest hunters was drowned within two miles from

the shore. Just what happened to him, we don't know. According to all appearances, he speared an oogruk or walrus, for his kayak was seen half capsized, full of water, and the inflated bag standing. He called for help and was seen on the ice giving signs of distress. Two boys ran to help as fast as they could. Shortly after two others started. They all got so excited that they never thought of pulling either the kayak or the bag. Finally the ice closed in and all disappeared.

"The name of the man is Ughitkuna, R.I.P. To allay the grief of the community, we rang the bell. After a short timely instruction we said Mass for the repose of his soul. The deceased leaves a wife pregnant and four children. Aolarana, his brother, was partly insane for about one hour. Such an accident brings home vividly the vanity of things of this world."

A sample of February, 1930, entry gives a good idea of the weather: "Mountains of snow fell during the night. The door of the shed was packed to the top. We had to shovel one hour to clear the entrance. However, the storm did not prevent one soul from coming to church."

From October, 1930, to June, 1931, Father LaFortune was in Kotzebue taking the place of the missionary who had been killed in the plane crash. He makes this entry in June, 1931:

"I came back to Nome to meet the Islanders. The summer was very bad in Nome. Hardly had the natives put their feet ashore when the flu pounced on them. They were coughing all summer. Six died and all the others were suffering. In spite of all, the natives worked unloading the boats."

Another entry having to do with conditions of health was made at the end of the same year. "Ever since we landed here, the weather has been favorable. There is no coughing to speak of, no tonsilitis, no serious toothache, no bad case of rheumatism. The hunting was fairly good. The case of medicine sent to me by Father Garasche proved to be a blessing. Some children who seemed to be in a bad way were put on their feet by the cod liver oil preparations."

One summer Father LaFortune and his Eskimo left the Island on a cutter and went to Nome. The umiaks were all piled in the forward hatch, and the priest was assigned to a room. After the captain went on deck to give commands, he came down to see if his guest was well taken care of. But Father LaFortune was not in his room, nor was he anywhere to be found. Later the Captain saw him in the forward hatch with his natives. There he was in his parka, his boots, his cap with visor, singing with them.

Once a visitor in Nome talked with the missionary and asked when he was going to visit the States. He looked at her. "Why, my dear child," he said. "I have nothing to go to the States for. There is nothing there for me." And he smiled indulgently as though anyone should think of such a question.

He takes no credit for anything, and his modesty is sweet and overpowering. Once in thanking a benefactor for woolen clothing that was sent to him, he said:

"After thirty-six years passed in this northern part of Alaska, I am inured to the cold. Even when I was a child, the cold of Canada did not affect me much. I froze my ears now and then, and that is all. Here in Alaska, in order to be in the swim with the others, I froze my cheeks and my nose, and every time, I came out of it with a brand new piece of skin."

Another incident reveals his meticulous consideration for his natives. Once when a plane stopped at the Island for a brief visit, the visitors were taken to see the community, for they were eager to buy some of the excellent workmanship. The tourists slipped into French while discussing the quality of the work. A swift, pleased expression broke over Father LaFortune's face, he heard his native tongue so seldom. But he immediately replied in English, mainly no doubt, because there were several ivory carvers standing there waiting, and he wanted them to know exactly what was taking place.

Father LaFortune knows his Eskimos as few others can know them. He speaks Eskimo, some say, better than they can. He is their adviser, he knows their needs. Once a visitor asked him what he would do if it were just time for Sunday mass, and walrus or whales approached his island. He quickly answered: "We would postpone the church services until the men and boys had their chance at hunting. Hungry people do not make good church-goers. Well-fed ones do, and anyhow they would then have something to be thankful for."

XIII

An Eskimo Village

HOOPER BAY warmed my heart from the beginning, but it was so far afield that I could not dream of visiting it. I felt I knew what it looked like, for each month, despite blizzard, mosquito plague, food shortage and overwork, a little mimeographed sheet called Hooper Bay News, *packed with warm, live word-pictures, brought us news of another land. It is harder than anyone knows (who has not tried it) to work up a monthly news letter, especially at a one-missionary station.*

THE ESKIMO DECIDES upon the site of his town by a set of standards peculiarly his own. He looks for a place near the water so that he can fish: if possible it will also have a seasonal supply of driftwood. Now at Hooper Bay the Bering Sea furnishes fish, and the Yukon and Kuskokwim Rivers bring down driftwood which the ocean currents distribute along the shore. The Eskimo does not mind living on a flat, marshy land, criss-crossed with streams, dotted with lakes and lagoons, where practically nothing will grow except berries. When the spring thaw almost buries him in mud, he simply puts on his long sealskin boots, and moves into a tent on higher ground. Nor does he mind the frequent cyclonic storms that breed in the Aleutian Islands during fall and winter and sweep up along the coast he calls his home. His life has always been like that.

The early missionaries visited the villages along the coast once or twice a year. They stopped long enough to baptize the children, give instructions, say mass, bring communion to the sick and do whatever else could be done during their few days' stay. Then they would go to the next village. Such an arrangement was a makeshift at best, and it was impossible to instruct the people adequately. Not until 1928 could a missionary be spared: Father Francis Menager was sent as first resident priest to Hooper Bay. Three years later, Father John P. Fox took his place, becoming priest, teacher, cook, sacristan, carpenter, mechanic and gardener. To these titles were later added marriage commissioner, reindeer herder, and postmaster. Hooper Bay is one of the larger Eskimo villages with a population of 307 natives, and out of the 800 in the district surrounding it, all but about 100 are Catholic.

Beside the work at the Bay, there are four stations over the tundra regularly visited by the priest: Scammon Bay forty miles north, Chevak the same distance northeast, Kashunak forty miles east, and Keyaluvik fifty miles further on. For the summer trips Father Fox uses a gasoline boat, and in winter a dogsled over the frozen rivers and snow-covered tundra. There is no road, automobile, or train to facilitate the trips.

We like to picture Father Fox on these visits calling his people to mass, making a complete circuit of the village ringing a little hand bell. During the winter the early morning is lighted only by the stars, while underfoot the crunch-crunch of the snow keeps time for the thin clear tinkle of the bell. It is already light during the spring mornings, and the impatient dogs growl and yodel as the missionary tramps through the wet, squashy village, the mud often flowing over the tops of his boots.

Each day's schedule is like that of the day before, and this is the sequence:

Rise at five, kindle the fires, make a round of the village with bell, say mass, visit the sick, teach school, have lunch, say breviary, do desk work, feed dogs, cut kindling for next day, do carpentering, lead rosary for children, eat supper, teach altar boys or conduct night school for men, hold common prayers for whole village, conduct singing class and give catechetical instruction for forty-five minutes. The plan varies on Saturday evenings by the addition of confessions, and on Sundays and feast days which call for benediction. There are a few other chores such as keeping the gasoline mission boat and other machinery in order, and running the thirty-two volt electrical plant which furnishes light for the mission buildings and for fifteen nearby igloos.

The conditions of the natives in the Hooper Bay area, from a civilized point of view, are bleak and desolate; and among the Eskimo, they are considered some of the poorest. In the village, floors are made of driftwood, but in the remote district there are no floors, little furniture, and all the family property is in the ten by twelve foot igloo, only six feet under the skylight at its greatest height. The skylight is made of intestines, not of glass. Away from the village, light and heat are still produced by a saucer filled with seal oil over which a rag hanging from the edge serves as a wick. Two families, or about ten people, ordinarily occupy one igloo. This is done not only to save fuel, but for economy of work in which two men of the family alternate: one of them hunts while the other gets fuel. Mostly the girl has no choice of a husband; her parents pick the one they think is a good hunter. Considering the poverty, cramped quarters, dirt floor, it is no wonder consumption is a commonplace.

When the snow covers the tundra, the wind blows great drifts over the village and all one can see of the igloo is a stove pipe protruding from the snow. Father

Fox said that the phrase "Dropping in on the family" must have been invented there for a dog team sometimes literally drops down through the skylight when all is covered by snow. Ordinarily one enters such a house by a long, narrow tunnel. It often means sliding in feet first, and coming out on hands and knees.

The lack of natural resources in these sections is one of the reasons for the Eskimo's poverty. North of the mouth of the Yukon there is coal, oil and gold. But in the section south of it where Hooper Bay lies, and as far as Bethel on the Kuskokwim, no valuable minerals have been found. The Eskimo, who live at and below Point Romanzoff, down to Nelson Island, are the least dependent of all on the props of civilization.

The Hooper Bay Mission in its fourteen years has added a few material comforts in the form of a light plant, radio, and mail delivery. Akulurak, 150 miles north, had formerly been the nearest post office. Sometimes friends brought the mail when they came from Mountain Village. Today, the monthly mail comes by dog team.

In 1928 at Kashunak Father Fox began training a group of native girls as interpreters, catechists, and housekeepers for the various missions. But with no financial help and without the stability which community life gives, this group did not prosper. Four years later, however, the missionary developed his idea further. At Hooper Bay he started a community of native women whom he called Sisters of Our Lady of the Snow. Anny Sippary, their Superior, was an expert cook, musician, sharpshooter, and could handle a dog team as well as a man. From the two charter members, the group by 1937 had grown only to seven: these first ten years were fraught with difficulties.

The year 1942, however, marks for them the beginning of a steady and permanent growth, for the very thing they have always needed is now being granted them: two Ursuline Sisters with Mother house at Festus, Missouri, have gone to Hooper Bay to train the native Sisters and to take care of the school. Their presence will give new life and stimulus, and will have far-reaching results.

The pre-missionary days of this Hooper Bay priest began at Uniontown, Washington, in 1892. After grade school he worked a few years and later entered Gonzaga University. During this time he thought in a general way of becoming a priest. Then, one of the Fathers offered him the life of St. Aloysius to read. Apparently, it did not appeal to him, for after struggling through a few pages, he returned the book. At this point the priest happened to ask:

"If you were on your deathbed now, what state would you wish to have chosen?"

His heart answered the question, and he chose the Jesuit way of life. Shortly afterwards he went home to get his trunk and to say goodbye. He said he knew nothing of the life of a Jesuit: he was afraid he would not be able to give a reasonable explanation of his choice, so he told no one of it.

He did his novitiate, juniorate, philosophy, taught

for two years at Seattle College, and was then sent to Spain for his theology. His interest in Alaska began through reading the Woodstock Letters from Alaska missionaries. This ultimately led to a request to be sent there.

He believes that the future of the missions depends entirely on what can be done for the young. The tribal superstitions are so deeply engrained in the adults that a priest can do little toward solid conversion by simply visiting their villages and teaching them. Although this is necessary too, the whole-hearted conversion of the Eskimo and Indians can come only by teaching the children in the schools. After a number of years of day to day training in the faith, they are apt to carry on after they leave school. Besides, many mission boys marry the mission girls, and lay the foundation of a really Catholic family.

Perhaps the greatest difficulty of the missionary is the scant financial help he receives. Mission organizations have long been helpful, but their assistance hardly covers more than the bare necessities of the missions. When a priest is already trying to do the work of two or three, he cannot effectively attend to the apostolate and support himself and the mission as well.

In the middle of the last century in France, a few servant girls began with pennies what later grew into the gigantic Propagation of Faith. Perhaps today we need a resurgence of this spirit. Enough sympathetic people could change the face of this poverty.

XIV

Angels Can Wear Parkas

*J*UST BEFORE I left New York near the end of April, an air mail letter came from Bishop Crimont. "Be sure to visit Sister Winifred in Port Angeles before you come up. She can tell you more in an hour than I can in a day."

Sister Winifred was tall and straight, and her years in the Alaskan wilderness had left no scars: she had young blue eyes in a young face, with a glowing radiance that made you think of wings and halos.

Sister M. Jules and her kitchen at Holy Cross Mission.

Sister M. of Perpetual Help, and Sister M. Eulalie,
Sisters of St. Ann.

Bishop Fitzgerald in winter clothes.

Bishop Crimont at work in Juneau.

A missionary's hut: where he eats, sleeps and works.

THE UPSHOT OF CIRCUMSTANCES following the martyrdom of the Archbishop founder of the Alaska missions in November, 1886, made it appear that all the moves had been planned ahead of time. The summer after that three Fathers and one Brother were working on the middle Yukon. And the summer following that one, Father Tosi arrived from the states with three Sisters of St. Ann. When these pioneer nuns stepped off the Yukon River boat at Koserefsky that August morning, the permanence of Holy Cross Mission was assured.

The three were Sisters Mary Stephen, Mary Pauline, and Mary Joseph Calasanctius. They soon became acquainted with Alaska weather, for they passed the first eight weeks of autumn not in a cabin, for none was ready, but in a tent. The story of those early years offered generally the same bitter winters, the same isolation, the same uninteresting food and poverty that continued through the following fifty-four until today. Some of the very first experiences, however, were too rare to have gone on happening, and must be at least summarily recounted here. They are chronicled in detail by Sister Calasanctius in *The Voice of Alaska.*

The Sisters' log cabin was made of freshly cut trees, and the occupants had to fill the cracks between the logs with a mixture of dry moss and clay. But forty below zero weather still found its way into the room, whereupon another precaution was taken: newspapers were pasted on the inside walls. Meanwhile strange noises filled the nights. First, the green wood exposed to the heat of the stove produced sounds like the crack of a rifle at close range. This was soon followed by the other extreme of sound: hushed, feathery, delicate disturbances—heralds of a plague of mice. They scampered over the beds all through the night, and ate the glue off the newsprint wallpaper. Though the mice were emptied out of the traps regularly, their numbers grew steadily, and battalions of them continued their nightly frolics. Then someone thought of making a novena to St. Gertrude. Suddenly, before the ninth day, the swarm mysteriously disappeared.

In the course of the next week Father Tosi casually mentioned that he had found a nest of mice in one of his shoes that morning. The army of rodents had changed their place of residence.

Six years after the arrival of that first group in Alaska, Sister Mary Winifred, a remarkable young Sister, came to Holy Cross and spent a great part of her life on the Alaska missions. She died only this year at Port Angeles, Washington. In the last ten years of her life she had not missed a day of teaching.

Around 1930 she suffered from an exceedingly bad throat and everything pointed to the end of her teaching career. So she asked the Little Flower to help her. Still the sore throat continued. She tossed the Little Flower's picture to one side, muttering crossly, "Why don't you cure me." And, immediately the answer flashed back to her: "Why don't you ask your patron saint?"

Thereupon Father Jette came to mind, for while at the mission school at Nulato, she had seen years of his heroic work among the Indians. Since his death in 1927 there had been nothing that she had needed. Now she appealed to him, and said:

"Father Jette, this is the first thing I am asking of you. Please do it for me. If you cure me, and the bad throat doesn't come back, I will say it is you who did it."

She did not stop at that. She turned to God Himself. "Now Almighty God," she said, "show that You appreciate all that Father Jette has done for You."

Her throat was cured.

Only a month before Sister Winifred died, she wrote a letter to Bishop Crimont speaking of the early days on the missions. She put on paper the same message that shone from her eyes when she spoke with people:

"I tell you in all sincerity that my love for Our Lord has grown more and more ever since [those early days in Alaska]. I feel no difficulty now in seeing Him really present in all my companions and in the children whom I teach. It is really Heaven on earth for me, and nobody can take this joy out of my heart. I feel Our Lord cannot hide from me any more, as He used to do, because I am always thinking of Him and finding Him in all His creatures."

Perhaps the inconveniences of isolation with its resulting conditions belong to the most severe hardships experienced in the wilderness. For the missions on the tundra are so far from medical help that even today the phrase "calling a doctor" has no meaning. Not long ago at Holy Cross a boy was shot in the chest while bringing down ptarmigan. The nurse sat by his bed day and night for two weeks, and though she could find no bullet, she was satisfied that it had not pierced his lung. After a few weeks the patient was well again. During epidemics, and indeed during other less serious times, the Sisters spend their days giving out pills, cough medicine, making the children gargle, washing out infected eyes, putting salve on running sores, and other such tasks. Many children die of "false croup," as well as of consumption. The care of a few dozen children in a very poor, wooden, old-fashioned dormitory presents difficulties not known in a modern well-equipped hospital.

In the past few years many collarbones have been fractured, legs and arms broken, fingers and toes half cut off. Efficient medical care was always readily given by a lovely young Canadian Sister of St. Ann. This nurse had been the mission's entire medical staff for some years.

Suddenly one evening in June of 1941 she came down with what seemed to be acute appendicitis. This was not like a mangled hand or a broken bone that could be taken care of at the mission. By the next day the mounting fever and pain were causing real alarm. The nearest railroad was some three hundred miles away, and the only regular transportation was the semi-monthly Yukon River boat. The only way, then, to get Sister

Mary Epiphane to the hospital and save her life, was to radio for a special plane. But the radio waves were ineffective that morning, and no outside station could be contacted. Late in the afternoon the operator at Flat finally caught the appeal and was just in time to reach the pilot of a plane which had landed nearby. The pilot temporarily deserted his three passengers and arrived a half hour later at the mission air field.

Meanwhile a delicate Indian boy, whom Sister had nursed through a serious illness, cried piteously at her departure. As her stretcher was being carried from the hospital to the rudely constructed truck, she was smiling, but pain was squeezing tears out of her blue eyes. She beamed at the boy's stuttering attempts to console her as he walked by her side. She pressed his hand and murmured:

"Oh, we all have to suffer a little for our sins."

Then she was lifted into the small plane, and no one expected to see her again. After a few weeks in the hospital, she was well again, and was trying valiantly not to show how she missed Holy Cross.

Another sizable hardship—one which might well be ranked above isolation—is drudgery. In the missions there is a light-hearted acceptance of hardship and poverty that is a twentieth-century lesson in living. They work hard at teaching, washing, cooking, mending, cleaning, sewing from morning until night; and they like it. Theirs is a happy, radiant life: it is Christianity on wheels.

Drudgery and poverty in the mission are with them

always, and not in flattering forms. The children are all clothed from the bags of contributors. Whole afternoons are spent in patching stockings, dresses and gloves; whole days in mending mukluks—native boots. To make them water-tight, they must be mended with round pieces of laftak soaked in water until they are soft. The odor of wet sealskin permeating the sewing room on such occasions is indescribable. The soles and sides of the mukluks continue to be patched until there is practically nothing left of the original. The Sisters put everything to as many uses as possible. They defilm the X-ray slides and use them instead of glass to cover pictures. They raise cats to catch mice, and when the cats grow old, use their woolly fur for the missionaries' mitten linings. They make doll parkas from the skin of mice to send to the states. Jelly is made from the bulb found beneath the wild rose flower (native name, Duduaks). The curled-up sprout of the young fern is used for salad. The tub for washing salmon is made from an old kerosene container. Most of the stoves are simple, home-made ones, starting out in life as oil drums, and since only wood is burned, no grate is needed. The missions are nearly self-sufficient communities. Flour, sugar, cereals, prunes and such staples must come from outside. It is well that they are self-supporting, since there is practically no money to buy necessities, and transportation doubles and triples the original cost of the goods.

To describe all the activities of the nuns would require a good-sized book. One of the important jobs, however, besides teaching the children, doing the community's housekeeping, taking care of the hospital, is the tending of the vegetable garden. Vegetables and fish supply most of the community's food. Because of the shortness of the season, the gardening is painstaking labor. In mid-February earth is placed in the oven to thaw and warm. At the end of the month, tomato, radish and lettuce seeds are planted in the dormitory. In April, when the ground is still white, these tender plants are transferred to the hothouse.

The schedule of the river ice varies slightly with the years. It usually begins to crack up by the sixth of May, and during the nights when it is still going by, the temperature remains below the freezing point. By the 26th of the month it has finished and the frost has come out of the ground. Then, such seeds as turnips and carrots are planted, and the plants which have already been started in the hothouse are transplanted to their new garden homes. These seedlings are given hats to protect them from the cold days still to come. Instead of the cans which were formerly used, the hats are now made of paper soaked with seal oil.

When the weeds begin to show, the smaller children under the direction of the Sister gardener don every imaginable kind of old dress and overall, and go barefooted to weed the garden, each trying to win the prize as best weeder. While the work is still in progress, the older girls are called to clean the hundreds of fish brought in each day from the nets and the fish wheels. August ushers in the berry picking season. Boys, girls, priests, Sisters, and Brothers brave the bears, mosquitoes and gnats, and come home at the end of the day with the year's supply of fruit pudding and pies as yet in the berry stage.

Before the middle of September the potatoes and other vegetables are sorted and sacked, and the crop begins to be stored in the cellar. The harvest of one of the recent years was 70 tons of potatoes, 6852 pounds of cabbage, 3500 pounds of turnips.

After the garden work is over school begins, and not far away looms the preparation for Christmas, when 245 pies are made, and 1600 biscuits and doughnuts. The original group of three Sisters grew through the years to eleven, and they never exceeded that number though at times they carried out the dual function of feeding and clothing 150 people as well as teaching the children how to carry on alone.

The Sisters of St. Ann were the first, and probably the most active, order of those serving the Missions for the natives in Alaska. However, others have done continuous work too; the Sisters of Providence from Montreal came to Nome in 1902, and today have a large, well-equipped hospital in Anchorage and in Fairbanks. The Ursuline Nuns teach the mission school at Akulurak, and until last year were at Pilgrim Springs north of Nome, and in the earlier years taught at Valdez and St. Michael. The St. Joseph of Newark Sisters were in charge of a hospital at Seward for a time, and now have a large one in Ketchikan. Today, however, both in the southern part of Alaska and in the interior, there are fifty-six Sisters representing seven religious orders.

There was once a convert priest who used to say: "Whenever I have been faced with various ways of life, I felt I must follow that way which contained the people I liked best. That always seemed a simple and foolproof test. And I always arrived at the same answer: the heroes of the world to me were those who cheerfully gave up their way of life, and were willing to give up their lives too for God. I know a Sister who spent years as a nurse in a leper colony; and I know missionaries to foreign lands who have given up all that an average man holds most important. If there is a way of life that draws such people, I want to follow it."

He must have known some Alaskan missionary Sisters too.

XV

Yesterday and Today

I FEEL *I should apologize for the inclusion of these modern missionaries since* Dogsled Apostles *is really a story of Bishop Crimont and as many of the early trail blazers as were needed to give a representative picture of the work. The present chapter really belongs to a historian specializing on the most recent phase of missionary work in Alaska: for him a great wealth of material is waiting.*

FREDERICK RUPPERT began life in San Francisco in 1879, spent most of his student days on the west coast, also in St. Louis, at Poughkeepsie, and in Naples. After five years in the ministry, he was made President of Loyola College in Los Angeles. Next he asked to be sent to Alaska. All this happened up to 1919 when he was assigned to Nome: it was the year after influenza had swept the Seward Peninsula.

There Father Ruppert's scholarly life underwent abrupt transition. Now he was a missionary living in a little frame house. Before the snow piled around its walls in the fall, there was no way to keep the wind from howling through the cracks. At night he had to put papers under and above the mattress, and use all the blankets and bearskins available. Still he had to fight all the night long to keep warm. But, when the snow piled up the houses were more comfortable. Each morning after fixing the fire at 5:30, he would kneel for one and a half hours motionless before saying mass. His breakfast was a handful of oatmeal, toasted on a pie pan in the oven. With it he would drink a cup of hot water. When on the trail he would eat what the Eskimo had: dried fish and walrus blubber. He would walk about in a heavy overcoat, Roman collar, high shoes with trousers tied in. His hands became all cracked open with cold; his face tinted from sooty fires showed signs of frostbite.

In summer the ground at Nome thawed only six inches down, so that the water had to be piped overground. As soon as the frost came all the pipes were drained and the water was delivered in pails. To get enough for cooking a scoop of snow would be used.

When the influenza epidemic swept over the country, whole native villages were wiped out. With so many Eskimo orphans needing a home, Pilgrim Springs Mission was begun ninety miles north of Nome. In the late summer the boat brought four Ursuline nuns to take care of the new Mission, and there on the beach awaiting the boat were the old sourdoughs of the town. Everyone who could get away from the cold had already left for the states and those remaining could well understand what the Sisters were facing. All were cultured women, one a fine pianist: they were to spend their first Alaskan winter less than a hundred miles south of the circle. After this brave and spectacular beginning, the Pilgrim Springs mission carried on for twenty-two years. It was only when driven to the wall for lack of funds that it had to be closed (temporarily, it is hoped). Money was not available to repair the dilapitated buildings, nor to build new ones.

Three years after the beginning of this mission came tragedy. On a blizzard-swept December day Father Ruppert with his dog team tried to get through to Pilgrim Springs with Christmas supplies. The missionary either unharnessed the dogs, or they broke loose, for the tracks showed that in a temperature thirty degrees below zero, the missionary pressed on alone for two miles, battling for his life against the raging blizzard. Some days later when one of his exhausted dogs appeared at Iron Creek, fifteen miles from Pilgrim Springs, a search was made.

They found the frozen body. Still standing guard over it was Mink, the lead dog who fiercely repelled those who came near, until he recognized the Brother who had fed it at the Mission. The dog was so starved he had eaten the fur lining out of Father's cap. That holiday season was indeed a sober and sad one for the whole community at Nome.

Meanwhile mission life went on. Another missionary came on to the middle Yukon to take the place of Father Jette who had gone: Joseph McElmeel, with smiling stern blue eyes, a ruddy complexion to match his life on the trail, and a square-set determination about his shoulders, came to Nulato which was to be his home for many years. Nulato was the starting point for all the stations within a radius of two hundred and twenty-three miles: Kaltag, Koyukuk, Galena, Ruby, Tanana. His coverage of these stations earned for Father the reputation of being the best musher on the Yukon. He built a chapel houseboat called St. Anthony, to solve the problem of reaching the Tena Indians in the summer at their fish camps. Among other things he developed the Mosquito league: and the Indians have adopted baseball with enthusiasm if not with speed. Father "Mac" is now Superior of all the Alaska missions and only the illness of Father Eline has made him for several years remain in Fairbanks while Father Baud carries on at Nulato.

In 1927 Francis Menager, of unique family record, first went to Alaska. Out of a family of fourteen who came from France in the early part of the century, three brothers became Jesuits, the other two serving for some time in Alaska, but Father Francis remaining there. Sent to Kashunak fresh from a chair in Philosophy in Spokane, he said he sank to his hips in mud when he took his first step in his new territory. It was not as yet an established mission. On leaving Seattle he had been given an organ which he brought with him. When his boat neared the village, he began to sing and play. After a two-hour concert, the natives were already his friends. People wore feather parkas made from black and white mud hens, and after each service the church looked as though it had been the scene of many pillow battles. As with many of the old time missionaries so with Father Menager: practically all his work has been with the Eskimo. After a year at Kashunak he began the mission at Hooper Bay: next he was sent to Kotzebue, Holy Cross, and Akulurak.

Through the middle twenties, the years rolled by with quiet serenity over the tundra, until a memorable day in June 1930 when the Marquette League presented to Bishop Crimont the first missionary airplane to be used in Alaska. It was called the Marquette Missionary. The Bishop said that coming across the country on its way to Juneau it hummed the praise of the

(*Photo by Maurice Sharp*)

You ought to see this under a pink-pearl sky.

(*Photo by Maurice Sharp*)

A house in Tanana on the Yukon.

The native children at Holy Cross weed the garden.

There is a ninety day growing season in the interior of Alaska.

League. This laymen's organization, under the leadership of the clergy, had just completed its twenty-fifth year of service for the Indian missions. Its charity had risen to great heights. During only eleven years it had raised $750,000 for them.

Piloted by Brother Feltes the Marquette Missionary arrived safely in Juneau. After that Father Delon, then Superior of the Alaska missions, with Brother Feltes as pilot and Ralph Wien as co-pilot spent a month covering over fifteen hundred miles and visiting all the principal mission stations of Alaska, a task that would have taken many months to cover by dog team. On the fateful flight, co-pilot Wien was at the controls. With him were Father Delon and Father William Walsh of Kotzebue. They were making a trial hop over that village before leaving for Nome. The plane took off as usual, the pilot circled the field once, but turned back and flew a mile at an altitude of four hundred feet. Then he throttled the motor for a turn, but when the ship was in the bank, it suddenly stalled. The motor nosed earthward and plunged straight toward the ground, burying itself to a depth where the ground is permanently frozen. The three men were killed and the plane was totally wrecked.

Shortly after this an activity of seemingly small dimensions began in the south of Alaska. A tiny island covered with spruce and hemlock in the Lynn Canal twenty-three miles north of Juneau was chosen as the new shrine site for the arctic home of St. Terese of

Lisieux. If you are there at sunset you can watch the Chilcoot mountains grow purple across the bay, and you try to figure out if this rugged little island silhouetted against a silver pink sky is real.

There was no money to begin the work, only a great confidence in the hearts of Bishop Crimont and Father William G. LeVasseur. Stone was gathered from the beach, sand and gravel were hauled from Mendenhall Glacier and Herbert River Glacier, logs were floated behind a tow-boat from the mainland to the island. Most of the work was done by voluntary help. Among those who donated their services were boat skippers, ex-pugilists, lawyers, teachers. The causeway was first built across to the island: this was a difficult engineering feat owing to the tides and severe winter storms. Next the retreat house and log cabins were built from logs cut out of the timber near Herbert River, and logged down the river to the bay. Today it is ready for summer retreats.

The scenery of the mainland and its tiny island is very beautiful. Each year in the late summer a large whale and her baby, their heads white on the sides, their bodies a shiny black, come into the harbor rolling and blowing water into the air. Often a mother bear and her cubs come within sight eating blueberries and salmon berries, but disappear when they see anyone watching them. In the nearby woods are the mule-tailed deer, and white goats with curly horns. There are great numbers of ptarmigan, grouse, and snowshoe rabbits. All kinds of salmon are plentiful there: king, cohoe, silver, humpies and dog. Many small yachts, and other fishing boats pass by. Wild game abounds. In the evening when the sun goes down beyond the snow-covered Chilcoot mountains, the spruce and hemlock gather close about the shrine.

Probably one of the most popular names connected with the Alaska missions today is that of the writer, lecturer, explorer and photographer known as the Glacier Priest, Bernard R. Hubbard, S.J. He has explored Alaska for the past sixteen consecutive years and has done more than anyone else to make its missions known over the country. One year he and his party spent the winter on King Island making many ingenious improvements and finally erecting a large bronze statue of Christ the King with hands outstretched toward Asia and America.

His first book, *Mush, You Malemutes* appeared as articles in the *Saturday Evening Post*. It is an excellent account of exploration in the interior of Alaska. Beginning at Nenana near Fairbanks he mushed over the tundra, southwest down the Yukon, doing reconnoitering flying in the little known volcanic sections of the Aleutian Islands, and going on foot over Taku and Mendenhall Glaciers farther south. His *Cradle of the Storms* is a thrilling account of the Alaska Peninsula-Aleutian Island area, where volcanoes are still changing the face of the earth, where rivers and valleys are transformed over night. In this region he found three of the largest active craters in the world, and predicted accurately the eruption of one of them, Mount Aniakchak. Once his plane was almost sucked into the burning depths of the pit.

Father Hubbard has taken many thousands of professional photographs of little known parts of Alaska, made sound pictures of the folk music and festivals of native tribes, and has given countless illustrated lectures over the country to raise money for the Alaskan missions.

XVI

"Liquidating" the Native

My TRIP up the Yukon told me that all was not well between the natives and many of the traders: later I learned that one coming by boat along the river could tell the route taken by a liquor-dispensing trader, for in his wake was desolation and drunkenness; that in some sections the Indian is in a state of economic peonage to the traders. I have sought advice in many quarters and hope that the following presentation may clear the air enough to bring the issue into the open.

FEW TRAVELERS to Alaska visit the country's interior and see the hunting and fishing culture of the native villages. Tourist agencies advertise the beautiful inside passage with its shore-line mountain ranges, some snow-clad, some purple in the dusk, and a few covered with glaciers like white icing overrunning a chocolate cake. But to reach the interior requires time. After you get as far as Skagway, you can cross the Alaska gulf, take a train north through the Alaska Range within sight of Mount McKinley, and after a day and a half, reach Fairbanks. But all this is civilized Alaska. Travelers want scenic wonders, and they are not disappointed.

In the real interior there are neither cities nor towns. The land is full of mountains and worn-down hills standing far back from the river valleys. The natives work at their fish nets and fish wheels in the summer; and in winter, except for a few who manipulate the fish traps under the ice, the whole family moves to its winter quarters where the hunter visits his trapline regularly. In spring the family returns to the village bringing to the traders an abundance of fox, muskrat, ermine and beaver. This is their life.

We speak here of the Indians along the great waterways of interior Alaska, the Yukon and the Kuskokwim Rivers and their many tributaries. But what is said of the Indians applies to the Eskimo as well, for the impact

167

of civilization on their ways of life has in varying degrees had the same effect. The innovation that has caused greatest damage to the native is the use of liquor.

The liquor traffic has always been a point of conflict between the clergy and the state in the history of colonization; and the problem has been serious from the earliest days of this country. One of the missionary Sisters observed: "It is so hard to do much for the Indians when there are three saloons within sight of the mission."

The casual traveler after seeing these native villages comes away with a profound sense of depression. Wherever the sale of liquor is permitted, on the Yukon or on Seward Peninsula, and Kodiak, or any other place, the results are the same. Furs are brought in at the end of the season, the trader evaluates them, and the native takes alcohol and food for the money that is coming to him. Natives have been known to spend over two hundred out of three hundred dollars worth of furs on liquor. Starvation rations were of course the lot of their families. These wilderness department stores, called trading posts, are filled not only with staples and simple foods, but with all kinds of expensive canned meats and other delicacies.

There is one healthy side to the picture, but it is one side only, and will not spread of itself. In 1940 the local people of Kotzebue pushed through the prohibition of liquor as sort of a local option. The Catholic Missionary and the doctor drew up a petition, and the town, almost to a man, signed it. As a result when their liquor licenses expired at the end of the year, the traders did not ask to have them renewed. Now Kotzebue is an Eskimo coast village north of Bering Strait and some two hundred miles northeast of Nome. A similar situation (allowing for differences of detail) prevails in a few of the native sections of Alaska. In most of the other villages in Alaska the stores are free to do as they please, since they operate under the laws of the Territory. However, individual villages differ: liquor is not sold on Little Diomede, King Island and Nelson Island where the stores are run by the Office of Indian Affairs. There are no stores of any kind in Hooper Bay and Akulurak. At Holy Cross no trader may settle on the Missions' ground without permission.

But there are yet flagrant cases where traders insist on dispensing liquor to the natives in the teeth of those who are trying to protect the natives. Some of the missionaries have made prolonged and tireless efforts to get the evil remedied, but up to date, their work has gone unheeded.

Diamond Jenness in *The Indians of Canada* has stated the problem succinctly, and what he says about the Indians in Canada applies to the Alaska natives:

Of shorter duration than diseases, because Europeans finally awoke to its menace, but while it lasted, almost equally destructive of aboriginal society, was alcohol. The Indians, unlike many other primitive peoples, had no alcohol beverage in pre-historic times, and from the earliest days of settlement they abandoned every restraint in their frenzy for the white man's firewater. . . . These excesses every trader and ex-

plorer observed throughout the length and breadth of Canada
down to the middle of the nineteenth century. Whiskey and
brandy destroyed the self-respect of the Indians, weakened
every family and tribal tie, and made them, willing or unwill-
ing, the slaves of the trading posts where liquor was dispensed
to them by the keg. Even the fur traders recognized its evils
and gladly supported the government when it finally prohibited
all sale to the Indians under penalty of a heavy fine.

It is particularly interesting to see just how the rem-
edy came to be introduced. Up to 1850 in the district of
James Bay, on Hudson Bay, the main article of the
Hudson's Bay Company's trade with the Indians was
rum. It was evidently disastrous to their morality, and
every Oblate Missionary did what he could to change
the situation, and to make it unlawful to give intoxicants
to the Indians; but nothing the missionaries could do
was of any avail. In that year, however, Father Laver-
lochere boldly decided that the situation could go on no
longer, and went to England to see the Director of the
Company. With documents and figures he showed the
commercial value of the Indian in producing fur. Then
he gave statistics of the decrease in furs over a period of
years. Then he produced statements showing the decrease in the number of Indians due to tuberculosis,
caused in turn by the excessive use of liquor. He demon-
strated that the Hudson's Bay Company was killing the
goose that laid the golden egg, and that by the free dispensing of rum, it was slowly killing the only group who
could do extensive and efficient trapping in such a
country.

As if by magic, the Hudson's Bay Company the following year prohibited any kind of liquors in its Indian trading posts, and later when Ottawa became the seat of legislation, the ban on intoxicants remained in force.

One would think that with such a precedent, the Alaska territorial government would pass a law prohibiting the sale of liquor to the natives, for it is that legislative body, rather than the United States government, who is responsible. But there are several factors which, up to the present time, have stood in the way.

Unlike the Indians in the United States, Alaska natives are considered under the law to have the same rights as white citizens. Some legal opinion holds that the Act of 1887 which prohibits the sale of liquor to Indians in the United States cannot be applied to the natives of Alaska, for in the United States the Indians are wards living on reservations. In Alaska, with few exceptions, there are no reservations, and since the villages are scattered along the thousands of miles of sea and river coastline, it would be difficult to determine Indian country in the accepted sense. Up to now, this interpretation has helped to prevent the application of the United States law to Alaska. There are others, however, who hold that the law may be applied. Those who are deeply interested in the welfare of the natives believe that there is a way to legislate on this subject wisely, and legally. They believe there should be no liquor stores in villages in which the preponderance of population is native.

The Liquor Lobby in Alaska is a power that stifles

the efforts of all groups working for the welfare of the natives. The Lobby successfully exerts a profound influence upon the territorial legislature to keep the supply lines open from the liquor distillers to the dealers and to the natives.

At present anyone can get a license to sell liquor in Alaska who has a sufficient number of signers on his petition. The Indian in some sections is really in peonage to the traders. If a trader wants to sell liquor the Indians either sign the petition or they get no supplies. One solution may be to have native cooperative stores in all the villages of the Interior. Another might be a law limiting the issuance of licenses to traders, and safeguarding the interests of the natives by suitable provisions in the law.

XVII
Salmon Fishing
(Food)

*J*UNE FISHING on the Yukon is a rare experience. I went down to the summer fish camp eight miles below Holy Cross, and accompanied the natives in their row boats, watching them gather in the gill nets heavy with fish, and disentagle the fighting, twisting red-gold salmon.

THE FISH and Wild Life Service have found that the life story of the Pacific salmon does not follow that of its Atlantic cousins. Each of the six species is different in its habits, but here we are considering only the king salmon (or Chinook), the most delicious as food.

The king salmon is happy in the north Pacific, and objects to living further south than the Columbia River. Various efforts to populate other waters with it have failed. After hatching at the headwaters of a stream, the young salmon learns to swim and frolic in its fresh water home: it knows no parents, for the Pacific salmon spawn only once, and die soon after. Anywhere from a few months to two years the salmon go out into the wide world, beneath the sun-lit ocean waves.

The adventure of the growing salmon in the ocean must be exciting and filled with hair-breadth escapes from the jaws of bigger fish. During these years they must often see companions disappear down the mouths of greedy monsters. Thus, their lives go on in a spacious world until they are four or five years old. Then, with unerring sense of direction, they find their way back to their own home streams. At this point the real hazards begin, for the white whales and lamprey eels make life miserable and uncertain for the king salmon returning to the scenes of their young fishhood. Some salmon escape with the tooth marks of the whale on their sleek sides. Others bear scars resembling printed characters on their shiny red-gold skin—the prints of the eel's rasping teeth. Those that survive the whales, eels, fish wheels, and nets of canneries and natives, make their way as fast as possible to their spawning grounds, averaging from 30 to 45 miles a day, and making the entire journey without food. It is thought that during this period of migration, their digestive juices do not function. On reaching the headwaters, they lay their eggs and die.

Though intriguing, the detailed life story of the Pacific salmon cannot be told here from the viewpoint of the salmon. This unfortunate fish must be considered only as nourishing food. The Indians say that when the bluebells bloom, it is time to put out the fish nets, and in reality as soon as the ice goes out of the mouth of the Yukon, the king salmon swims up against the current. To catch these delicious first arrivals, averaging around twenty-five pounds each, the Indians have long used a primitive type of gill net. Those used today are made of linen twine. In early June a Brother, a young Scholastic and a group of older native boys row some eight miles down the river to the summer camp. There they live in tents during the fishing season, each day getting large supplies of fish to feed some 150 hungry mouths throughout the year.

On arriving at the fishing grounds they put the gill net into a favorable spot in the river. One end is secured by a long shore line to a tree: the other end is anchored by a heavy rock at right angles to the shore. Like a net on a tennis court, it remains fairly erect under the water, for there are sinkers attached to the bottom, and pieces of wood as floaters attached to the top.

When a current is strong at the bend in the river near the shore, there will be an eddy or current flowing upstream on the other side of the bend. Into such a strong eddy the net is set, for no salmon would be caught if it were placed in a regular current. The fish fighting their way upstream are necessarily swimming slowly. If they see a net bulging out in their direction, they can slow down to avoid it. But the behavior of an eddy makes this unlikely, for the back current causes the net to swing upstream. When a salmon enters an eddy, its speed is greatly increased, for from fighting against the current it is rushed along with it. When the fish sees the net just ahead, it is too late to swerve, and its own speed carries it on. The mesh of the net—about six to eight inches wide—catches the fish behind the gills and in its mad struggle to get away, entangles many strands of the cord about its body. Only the smaller king salmon can wriggle their way to freedom.

Those first fish taken from the net are fat and red and luscious; those at the end of the run contain less oil, and are often bruised and battered as though their journey was one continuous struggle.

But the catching, once the nets are in, is only one step. Cleaning and preparing the fish is an important part of native and mission economy. Through the season various groups are made responsible for the work: either a shift of older boys with a prefect and Brother in charge, or the older girls with a Sister supervising and working along with them. Part of the cleaning takes place at the fishing camp, but most of it is done at the mission after the boat brings the daily supply from the camp.

In cleaning the king salmon, the head is first removed. It is a common practice among Eskimo and Indians to put the discarded heads of the fish into a hole to rot. When the heads have reached a more or less advanced state of decay, the natives retrieve them and eat them as they are. The children say that uksunuk (rotten fish heads) are better than candy. That is a matter of taste. It is interesting to know, however, that Eskimo who have been offered a taste of limburger cheese, regard it with as vigorous disdain as the white people regard the decayed fish heads.

After the head, the bowels and eggs are removed; then, with the aid of an extremely sharp knife and several deft strokes, the backbone is cut out. Next, if meant for salting, the fish are cut into square pieces. But, if salmon strips are desired, the halved fish is laid upon a table and cut into long strips about an inch wide. These are placed in brine for some minutes, then hung up on poles in the air to dry. After several days they are hung in the smokehouse to be thoroughly smoked. There the excess oil in which they are so rich, drips out. This process dries them completely and preserves them indefinitely. The strips, sometimes called Yukon candy, are delicious to the most fastidious taste, and can be eaten any time during the year.

After king salmon, dog salmon, weighing about eight pounds each, come up the river. Although principally used as dog food, these also supplement the better kind of fish for natives and missionaries. These can be caught in great numbers in the fish wheel, an apparatus first known on the Tanana River around 1905. Gradually through the years, the fish wheel has increased the catch of the nets, especially on the middle Yukon at and above Holy Cross where the Indians—rather than the Eskimo—live.

These wheels are constructed of laths and chicken coop wire, and range around 18 feet high. They are set in the edge of the river, and the strong current revolves them. A large wooden box fastened on the surface of the water to the wheel's structure, catches the fish which slide off the slanted shelves within the wheel as it revolves.

During the run of dog fish two of these wheels might well average 1,000 fish a day. But, considering that each dog eats one dry dog fish a day, and sometimes, when working hard, even more, and considering that especially in lean years, these dog salmon must furnish a good part of the food for people, this supply is not too plentiful.

The food the native eats depends on what kind of a year it has been. If hunting has been good, they eat much meat: if trapping has been good, they have money to buy plenty of flour and some vegetables. But, if the year has been a lean one, the natives might well depend on dried dog salmon for one regular meal a day. And on every trip they make in winter or spring, dog salmon is the main food.

After cleaning, the flesh of the dog fish is cut on both sides of the backbone and around it, leaving the halved fish joined at the tail. A double pointed stick is inserted crossways through the sides, holding the inside of the fish open to the air. They are then placed on long poles to dry, after which they are put into the smokehouse for the longer process of smoking.

Fishing by gill nets and wheels goes on through the early summer. A completely different method is used during the winter months, when a smaller kind known as whitefish and lush are sought. The long cold nights and the shorter daily circuit of the sun herald the approach of the winter fishing season. After the river freezes the natives make a funnel-shaped basket about eight feet long and three feet wide, using spruce tree roots and tying the joints together with willow bark. The traps are set out during November or December, the catch being fairly constant during the whole winter until April.

These baskets are ingenious contrivances and worthy of detailed description. It is said that the Eskimo methods of hunting the sea mammals were taken from the more ancient methods of hunting land animals, and of fishing in the lakes and rivers. Certainly, the natives have shown great intelligence in their ways of procuring food.

Imagine a huge bullet-shaped object made of wicker-work. The small end of the trap has an opening about a foot wide with a little door made of the same wicker-work that will swing open when one small wire is removed. Inside the basket are rounded hoops lashed tightly to the main body with pliable thin lengths of green willow wood. These hoops are made of evenly whittled strips of bent spruce wood with their two ends lashed together. This gives them roundness and stability. The spruce tree roots are split into long thin strips by the aid of the native's teeth and a knife. They are fastened lengthwise about an inch apart, from front to back of the trap, and lashed to the three or four hoops which form the framework. All the tying is done with thin strips of willow split in the same way as the spruce roots.

Before the trap is lowered, a main fence is put down into the water and one end is fastened to the shore or sandbar. The other end is fastened to long poles driven into the soft river bottom, these poles forming the outer structure of the basket. All these contrivances provide a complete directive route for the fish. I am told that one who has not done the work cannot realize the torturous job of putting in that fence, of cutting the long trench in the ice, and of tying the fence together in sub-zero weather. Water splashes and freezes on clothes, hands, and shoes, but the bitter cold work goes on.

Now having chopped out a rectangle of ice large enough to put the trap into the water, it is lowered to a depth of several feet below the ice. Finally, after the lighter and heavier poles are fastened securely, the basket is ready to catch the fish.

If the fish are running thick, one hundred or so each day will be caught; each time the natives must dig down in the ice to lift up the basket. The trap is then raised out of the water, the big end is opened and a bag two feet long lashed to a long pole is used to get the fish out. The fish are scooped on to the ice where they freeze immediately. With all their summer and winter fishing, the natives still go hungry at times, for there is great fluctuation in the quantity of fish from year to year.

XVIII

Reindeer and Caribou

(Clothes)

*S*OME WILD-LIFE *people told me they remember seeing caribou trails along the ridges around the Ididerod River as late as 1910, trails that had been beaten down through the centuries. They were about twenty-four feet wide and of varying depths: some places would be tramped down to bedrock. Yet at that time there were very few caribou in that vicinity.*

My first interest in the domesticated cousin of the wild caribou came from hearing stories about Smoozie, *a reindeer fawn at Holy Cross.*

TO UNDERSTAND THE REINDEER in Alaska, one must go back to the time when the Arctic belonged to the land and sea animals and the Eskimo claimed only enough of them to keep his family in food and furs. This economy was balanced by nature until the middle of the last century, when the whalers disturbed it. They found large numbers of whales, countless herds of walrus and other sea animals. Slowly the animals moved farther north beyond the zone of danger, which also meant beyond the reach of the natives. The seal was being slowly exterminated, too, and the Eskimo had to tramp fifteen to twenty miles over the ice before he could reach one. The modern hunter with his gas and steam launches and rapid-fire guns had found all these sea animals. The natives no longer enjoyed a supply of whalebone, ivory walrus tusks and sealskins. These they had always used as a means of barter with Siberian traders from whom they obtained reindeer skins to keep warm.

Dr. Sheldon Jackson, general agent for the government schools in Alaska at that time, saw the danger signs. The natives were finding it more and more difficult to get food and clothing, and actual years of scarcity were weakening the race. When he found that the Chukche tribe across the Bering Strait in Siberia had no years of famine, he inquired into its cause. They were a hardy race: though their climate and living conditions were similar to those of the Alaskan Eskimo, there was only one difference between the two ways of life. The Chukches owned herds of domesticated reindeer whose presence insured a stable life. It made the difference between a prosperous people and those who often went half-fed. Thus the importation of reindeer was brought about to give economic stability to the natives. And the increase of the reindeer herd would soon become an added source of revenue.

In 1890 the government brought the first deer into Alaska. During the first ten years 1,260 head were imported. Small herds were loaned to the missions which agreed to train Eskimo as herders, others were distributed among the natives. A number of Laplanders and their families were brought over by the government to train these Eskimo apprentice herders. The natural increase in the herds early in the present century had brought the number of deer to 6,000. They were scattered in herds from Point Barrow to Bethel on the Kuskokwim River.

Their new home was barren tundra where no horse, cow, sheep or goat could find pasture. But deer could be turned loose on the tundra to forage for themselves. There they found a great variety of food: they eat all kinds of Arctic grasses and shrubs in the summer, and reindeer moss in the winter. At different times of the year they showed a special choosiness about their food, eating duck and goose eggs, and occasionally devouring nest and all.

Into this apparently happy picture crept a thing

which took on more significance through the years, that is the deep-seated and century-old dislike in the bosom of the Eskimo for staying in one place throughout the year. His inherited customs prompted him to move to the coast for fishing and hunting sea mammals in the summer, and to move to a winter camp when the cold set in. The stabilizing influence of a herd of reindeer that had to be continuously taken care of was entirely new and looked on by him with a great deal of suspicion. In this the Chukche tribe, which is not truly Eskimo but of Indian blood, differed from the Eskimo. They were willing to stay in one place and herd the deer.

When fawning days come in the spring the herder gives the deer meticulous care. His instinct prompts him to sit on top of a rock to look over the sea for whales using the binoculars he gets from the whaling ships. But he cannot afford to do this: he must give the deer his every attention. At fawning time the does must have good grazing, with coves and hollows and available patches of protecting brush or timber. The babies are usually born on some portion of the summer range, on the exposed flats along the beach, or on the south slopes of the hills nearby. The snow leaves these areas early, exposing patches of bare tundra where the does find the first fresh growth of succulent green feed. The sun must be of melting warmth in the day, and much colder at night. If the water running over the feeding grounds freezes solid, the mothers may starve to death. Also when it is slippery the does may walk around and break their legs. Many other dangers lie waiting for the baby deer. Sometimes the new fawn might die from freezing. If the herder and his dog are not always on the watch, the wolves will chase the does away from the fawning grounds and the babies will die of starvation. Fawning season is not the only time when the herder is necessary. When the forage becomes eaten out, then the herder must move the deer some fifty miles away to a new location where food is plentiful.

Now the importation of the reindeer was not like introducing a new kind of animal for the Eskimo to take care of. The reindeer is actually the domesticated cousin of the wild caribou which roamed over northern and central Alaska in herds of thousands. In the latter part of the last century, men prospecting for gold killed great numbers of caribou for dog meat. And as the years went by and the mining, fishing and trapping activities in Alaska increased, the herds of wild caribou became harder to find. So it was not only the new developed scarcity of whale, walrus and seal that made life difficult for the Eskimo, but the gradual disappearance of the plentiful caribou from their old haunts.

Little is known about the annual migrations of the caribou, but enough to show that they frequent the coast in summer to escape the mosquitoes that infest the woodlands: they also lick up the salt deposited by ocean waters. In the fall they travel to the mountain regions further south. They follow the same track indefinitely unless something occurs to make them change.

Thus, for instance, if the moss has either been eaten or burnt off, or tramped down, they will vary their line of march. On Seward Peninsula places can still be recognized where the natives used to drive the caribou down into the water to kill them.

The caribou and reindeer with variations have the same general characteristics. The caribou is generally lighter in color, has longer legs and is more ungainly than the reindeer. They are the only species of the deer family in which both sexes have antlers. Even the fawns have little knobby branches in their first year. The first few months the antlers, still covered with a reddish black velvet, are soft and easy to break. This covering is a downy fur about two-thirds of an inch long. By November or December the velvet is scraped off: sometimes it still hangs about their heads in loose shreds. Beneath, the horns are hard, and of a brownish color. In the fall when the deer are being roped and marked in the corral, unless great care is taken, the fawns might break their soft tender horns.

If the deer have had a quiet summer their horns are larger, but if the flies and mosquitoes have been bad, the deer will be less strong, and their horns less developed. The tundra is covered with pools and small lakes made by the melting snow. As the ground is frozen a few inches solid below the surface, the subsoil does not absorb the water, and the pools remain all the summer as breeding places for mosquitoes. They are truly an annual plague for both man and beast.

The branching of the horns of the adult reindeer is

irregular, and is different in every deer. They curve
back and then swing forward. Often in the autumn the
bulls fight each other, rushing full speed from some
little distance and meeting in a head-on collision. Sometimes as a result of the clash, they lock horns and cannot
disentangle them. Several years ago a pilot flying over
the Alaska range saw two deer fighting, and he circled
down taking moving pictures the while. By the time he
had landed his plane and came near to the deer, their
horns had locked so that they could not go on fighting.
He rescued them by cutting them apart. A few hunters
have found locked antlers on the tundra without their
owners. No doubt wind, weather and wolves accounted
for the bodies. Once a deer with a dead wolf impaled on
his antlers became so weak from the weight of the body
that he could not go on. Finally a hunter found and
freed him. The horns are shed in spring and fall according to age and sex. The outside of the horn does not
slip off like the skin of a snake, but the whole antler,
which has now become very tough-boned, breaks off.

The reindeer have eyes which are large and confiding
and gentle. Their fuzzy nozzles are more like those of a
cow than the pointed delicate nose of an ordinary deer.
Their hair is short like that of a horse, except the hair
on their legs which is long, and which furnishes the
Eskimo extra protection for his mukluks. Their ears
are not big like other deer, nor do they have a long thin
neck. Their neck and shoulders are a graying white,
darker on the back, shading into a much darker color
on the sides of their abdomen and hindquarters. White

deer, contrary to common report, are generally smaller and less robust, and are thought to have bad eyes. They tire easily, and are a prey to wolves who track them down without trouble.

In cold weather the steam rising from the herd makes them appear from the distance a slow, grey movement. The steam which is thought to come both from their bodies and from their breath, can be seen long before the outlines of the herd themselves. When crossing streams, reindeer swim high out of the water, especially the adults, because of their hollow, buoyant shafts of hair.

The deer have as a sixth sense a power of orientation which draws them back to their range from any point to which they are taken. They also have a keen sense of smell which enables them to detect mosses buried deep beneath the snow. They are extremely gregarious, and become very lonely and frightened when by themselves. The reindeer and caribou both have a wide hoof that seems designed especially for the Arctic wilds. The width prevents them from settling down into the damp snow, and into the swampy soil, and its sharpness enables them to run on ice readily and without slipping.

When a few deer become frightened, they quickly regain the herd. But when the herd is frightened, or hears the barking of wolves, or when their leader has not definitely started one way, or if they are under some other pressure, they begin to mill. In some sections they mill clock-wise; in others counter clock-wise. If they are attacked by wolves they are said to protect them-

selves by the furious use of their large hooves in addition
to their antlers. Often, the wolf will try to separate one
deer from the herd, then by means of his tireless, patient
gallop, he will wear down the deer until it can go no
further. Then he will either tear at its throat, or ham-
string its legs, or tear out its tongue. At the time the
reindeer were introduced into Alaska there were practically no wolves in the country, except on the Arctic
Coast, and in the direction of Canada where the caribou
were plentiful.

The domesticated reindeer were introduced into
Alaska at the turn of the century for one purpose: to
furnish for the Eskimo a less precarious existence. By
1915 there were supposed to have been 600,000 reindeer in the country. Meanwhile during the intervening
years, 100,000 additional ones had been used for food
and clothing. An estimate without an accurate count
made it seem that natives owned two-thirds of the
600,000 deer.

Around 1918 at the time of the influenza, the deer
were closely herded, each herd containing less than one
thousand deer: but in the late twenties, the size of the
herds began to change. The people reasoned that if the
range was too small, the deer trampled the moss. So
for the time the period of close herding ended, and the
reindeer were allowed to run loose. When there was to
be a killing for meat or fawn skins, the herders would
chase the deer into a corral.

Through the years many plans have revolved about

A future team.

The government freight and passenger boat makes two trips each
month on the lower Yukon.

(Photo by Father Hubbard)
The weather places difficulties between an Eskimo and his food.

(Photo by Father Hubbard)
An air raid warden at Kotzebue

the reindeer industry. At one time a slaughter of the deer at Kokrines on the Yukon was contemplated. The meat was to be dressed, frozen, and sent by barge to Nenana, then placed in cold storage for exportation via Seward and steamer lines to Seattle. It was hoped that reindeer steaks might become accepted for regular use in the states. It was further estimated that the 200,000 square miles of treeless region in northern and western Alaska which could not be used for agriculture, would furnish pasturage for four million reindeer. Despite all this, the content and strength of the reindeer meat as well as the high cost of freight, made the plan impracticable.

The quality of the meat is still a mooted question. Many consider it unfit for hard-working people, those who need strength-giving foods. Perhaps as a food reindeer meat will be but supplementary during years of scarcity. There is no doubt but what the industry, supervised and developed entirely for the benefit of the natives, will be of great value to them. The reindeer sinews can be used for skin sewing; the adult hides for native mattresses, sleeping bags, fur socks and waterboots; the fawn skins for parkas, caps, cold-weather pants; the legs for fur boots and mittens; the horns for handles of implements. Deer pull sleds successfully in various other Arctic countries, but they have never challenged the place of dogs in Alaska.

September, 1937, ushered in a new era for the domesticated reindeer. The Alaska Reindeer Act authorized the government to purchase all these animals which were owned by others than natives of Alaska, later to be distributed to the natives under some provision which would insure their future economic security. Thus Congress adopted a policy eliminating all participation in the reindeer industry of Alaska by whites.

Charles G. Burdick of the Alaska Forest Service headed a staff which made an exhaustive survey by airplane of the reindeer country, making an actual count of the animals at the various corrals. This resulted in the purchase by the government of 82,538 reindeer at an average price of $3.98 apiece. What had happened to all the other deer thought to have been under white ownership is still a mystery. The fact that the total number of the deer was only 82,538 was determined by accurate and scientific counting. The earlier estimates of ownership had not been based on actual count. Some thought that many thousands had been killed by wolves, also by starvation in the winter of 1938–39, the severity of which produced deep snow and glaciation of many of the ranges. Probably the biggest factor was the costly mistake of the later twenties, that is, the notion that reindeer did not need herding. Experience has now taught that when herding ceases the reindeer becomes wild and mixes with the caribou. After a costly lesson the pendulum has now swung back.

The Reindeer Service plans a healthy constructive policy, including herding, selection of adequate pasturage, grazing areas, annual round-ups, marking, castrating and butchering. Reindeer are no longer the exclusive property of Santa Claus: they are coming into their own.

XIX

Eskimo Dogs

(Transportation)

I MET MY first Eskimo dog in Central Park in New York—it was a bronze statue of the famous Balto, dedicated to the sled dogs that in 1925 brought the toxin six hundred miles over rough ice and snow through Arctic blizzards from Nenana to Nome.

My first live malemute acquaintances lived along the Yukon and were less impressive: the poor fellows were tied up by the river's edge leading unhappy, idle lives all through the summer, growling and longing for the time when they might howl at the moon like wolves and fly over the snow in their glee.

ONLY IN THE ARCTIC countries do dogs rank highest among animals in usefulness, for without them the Indian and Eskimo would be lost. The breed is thought to be heavily crossed with the wolf which strongly resembles these dogs in appearance and in voice. When disturbed at night they have a peculiar weird howl almost like yodling; sometimes it resembles an oriental tune in soprano, and at other times the sound of a baby crying.

The bigger dogs, weighing some seventy pounds, are called Malemutes. The Siberian husky, somewhat smaller, weighing only about sixty-five pounds, is very tough. This dog can be recognized by the size of his feet, by his big, tough-looking head. Some have a pretty face like a police dog, others look formidable. The hair is sometimes yellow, sometimes black and white, sometimes wolf grey, sometimes spotted. Because of the need of warmth they are equipped with a heavy, coarse top coat which takes on a softer finer texture beneath. But their individuality in appearance and in action knows no bounds. Each one is supremely unpredictable.

The dogs are used in northern and central Alaska by everyone—this means the native, the trader, the trapper, the miner, the missionary—for sustained winter transportation. Their only rival is the airplane. Training begins when the dog is about five months old, when it is two-thirds grown or, if possible, earlier. If he is to be a work dog, he is merely put into harness. But training a lead dog is a delicate job calling for skill on the part of both trainer and dog. The black snake whip is used only to frighten, not to beat him.

Jiggs was an Alaskan lead dog known for his personality. He was a mixture of light grey and white spots, also a mixture of stubbornness and sagacity. When he was being trained he did not like to keep the towline taut. This is the center line that pulls the sled. It is connected by a short line to the harness and neck of each dog except the leader. Behind the leader are two swing dogs abreast, then come two more in the middle; in the back are two wheel dogs nearest the sled. On its oak runners which extend in the back, the musher stands. Beside him extending from the middle of the sled is an iron brake.

On some of the trial trips Jiggs would look back at the driver with his ears straight aloft. At first he would lie down when he got tired, or until he was frightened with the whip. Finally he began to learn that "gee" meant right, and "haw" meant left. If anyone but his master tried taking him on the trail, he would do everything to defeat him. He would run away; or run into anything he could find. He could be full of fun one minute and in the midst of a ferocious fight the next. As with many other dogs, it was his hobby to attack anything that was running. But he was not mean, and would never hurt a child.

It is said that a driver must be extremely tough and firm in teaching his dogs. The story is told of an amateur musher who got his team together, hitched them up, loaded his sled, and stood on the back calling to the dogs to start. Instead of starting, the leader circled around, came back, and licked his face.

This story could never be told of Jiggs, for he had too much wolf in him. Jiggs took his responsibility as leader very seriously, and would allow no insubordination on the part of any of his team. Once on a long trip Tinker, one of the swing dogs, bit him. But Jiggs knew he had to get to his destination that night, so he took no time for discipline on the road. On reaching the village at eleven o'clock that night, the driver began to unhitch Jiggs in the darkness. Jiggs immediately turned around, got the towline taut so the other dogs kept away from each other, then proceeded to give Tinker a good lashing. Tinker's ear was slashed and there was a big piece of flesh out of his right leg. Jiggs looked up at his master and wagged his tail as much as to say, "Well, I guess you understand; I had a job to do."

Jiggs' sagacity was always a joy to his master. When two teams met on the trail, a terrific snarling and yelling would begin instantaneously if the dogs passed near each other, and it would continue until ended by the drivers' whips. If properly trained, the leader will swing his dogs out at right angles from the trail and wait until the other team has passed. Jiggs did this with great pride and deliberation, but with all his bright helpfulness, he could never withstand the temptation to run after a cottontail if one crossed his path. His musher on such occasions would have to apply the brakes heavily.

But what he lacked in temperament, he made up in instinct. He would recognize a trail he had been over years before even though it was covered with layers of snow and ice. There was a case where nobody had been over the trail for years, but Jiggs swung around, then took the dogs over the portage and came out exactly at the same place where the original trail ended. Once when lost in a storm, the men on the sled had no way of knowing the direction, and were trying to force the dogs over to the right. But, finally, knowing they were lost, in desperation they let the dogs go their own way. They arrived home safely in the middle of the night.

Jiggs was full of mischief. He would run away whenever possible, would lead toward home, and take the whole team with him. The least sign of activity would throw him into spasms of glee. With his mates he would bark, howl and roll in the snow. Then, when hitched to the sled, the dogs would prick up their ears, fling their tails in the air, and start at breakneck speed. Many winter days the woods were magnificent, the dark pines weighted down with ridges of pure white snow; in late afternoon the sinking sun would cast a pink tint over the rolling white blanket, and slowly along the foot of the slopes the pink would change into a deep purple. At the first bend the rider might be thrown ingloriously in the twinkle of an eye into the deep snow.

Sledding at night is a glorious experience. If the load is light, the musher might lie down on the sled and let the dogs run at will without calling to them. Filled with a seeming sense of their own responsibility, they would yip and howl at the moon like wolves, and literally fly over the snow in their glee.

Jiggs had an innate honesty along with his sense of mischief. Every evening each dog was given a fish for its day's rations. One time while the other dogs proceeded to eat their fish, he quickly buried his. When the boy came around again to give the unserved dogs their fish, not remembering that Jiggs had already had his, he gave him another. Jiggs quickly uncovered his buried fish, picked it up between his teeth and looked up at the boy.

A driver soon learns his dogs' habits. If the dog has not eaten all the fish, he might stay awake all the night guarding it. Or he might wake up and finish it in the morning. This must be avoided for the dog should have only water in the morning.

One of Jiggs' famous escapades was the time when he and the team got loose, and after a hilarious day over the countryside, came home at night howling piteously. They had run into a family of porcupines. Quills had pierced through their skin, gotten into their mouths, and into their tongues. They were very sad indeed. With the use of chloro-liniment, cheesecloth, a quantity of strong rope, knife, pliers and scissors, eight dogs were operated on successfully, and most of the squills removed. But Jiggs, stubborn and proud even in his pain, stayed at a distance. Three days later he came in looking woe-begone. The quills had festered in his skin, and he was finally subdued into letting something be done for him.

His sense of vigor and pride made him difficult in

other ways too. Often when several crusts of ice formed
one over the other, each freezing solidly, the result
would be a series of sharp-edged layers which cut
through the pads of the dogs' paws. When this happened, their feet were likely to bleed. Sometimes it
became necessary to lay them up. Little boots made
of outing flannel or canvas or soft leather also afforded
protection. On such occasions Jiggs would act as though
the footgear were an insult to his prowess, and would
not be content until he had maneuvered the shoes off.
At times the ice formation was so sharp and hard and
the dogs' feet got so bad that the driver would have to
walk back home on snowshoes, pulling the dogs in his
sled. Sometimes balls of ice formed between the dogs'
toes, and these the musher would carefully remove with
his fingers.

The problem of dog food is a difficult one when long
trips are undertaken. Fish is the best strength-producing
food, but cooked rice and bran and oatmeal are also
serviceable. A good team of dogs can pull two or three
hundred pounds, but if it is to be a long trip, perhaps
one-third of the load might be dog food, especially if
food cannot be procured on the way. With a load like
this the musher must run on snowshoes in the back of
the sled helping push it when the dogs are laboring.

In these summer days practically all the traveling is
done by boat or plane; consequently the dogs are given
less food. In the early days prospectors used dogs even
in the summer for trips into the interior where a boat
could not be used. With winter the dogs come into their

own, and their joy at getting in harness again is over-
whelming.

One of the really dangerous situations that requires
steady nerves on the part of both driver and dog leader,
is the presence of running water a short distance away
from the trail. Sometimes the swift current of the Kuskokwim is open until the middle of January. These
angry waters have occasionally swallowed up musher,
sled, dogs and all. A sudden swerve of the sled on the
wind-swept ice or a misdirection of the leader could
bring disaster. But the leader seldom gets jumpy on such
occasions. He most often has a sixth sense for water.
Jiggs was so proud of his sensitiveness to water that
even when he came to a tiny, harmless brook, he would
stop grandly a few seconds before crossing.

The natives give little consideration to the treatment
and welfare of their dogs. In the native villages they are
tied up along the waterfront in the summer, and at the
approach of each boat, they howl and bark viciously
and continuously. If let loose they would destroy everything in the village. They seem to suffer both from the
weather and from their inactivity. They appear hot,
miserable and bad tempered.

Before white men came into the country, natives
used to tie the dogs up in the summer with a long fork-
shaped stick. The dog's head was in a triangle, the
other end was tied to a post. This was the only way to
keep him from biting through the leather or through
the rope. Today chains and heavy ropes thirty or forty
feet long are used. Unless the rope is very heavy, the

dogs will eat through it and get into a fight with each other.

Usually white mushers become very fond of their dogs. When leaving the country they are careful to leave the dogs with somebody who is kind to them. After ten years of hard work a dog is stoved up and is no longer much good. The natives, on the other hand, are usually short of food, and when a dog gets old, they kill him. The two mushers in Jiggs' life became extremely fond of him, but they are both gone from the country now. Jiggs is an old dog and though he has lost some of his fight, he still leads with the same pride and skill.

XX
Ways of Life:
Alaska versus America

WHEN I found myself suddenly surrounded by a completely strange culture I got so many impressions of the natives that none of them were clear—their idioms, their pleasing voices, their clear bronze skins, the dancing Eskimo eyes, their intimate knowledge of animals, their readiness to be friends. Slowly the impressions sorted themselves out. Next I began noticing the great amount of coughing, the many cases of what they call false croup, a mouth of sparkling teeth, next to one with many decays. Then I began to make inquiries, and this chapter is the result. I found that scientists carrying out experiments in Alaska have developed knowledge of great value not only to the natives, but to our own civilization.

THE IMPACT OF AMERICAN culture upon the Alaskan native culture shows up our own in a new and critical light. The meeting of the two has not always been either to the credit of the stronger or the benefit of the weaker.

Consider, for example, the inroads that "civilized" diseases made into the Eskimo country! Even our mildest diseases proved at first fatal to the unimmunized natives. The isolation of the Eskimo until the 20th century deprived them of all medical services. Today, many survivors have developed a partial immunity to the commonest diseases, and the government has established centers with doctors and nurses to check the spread of epidemics and combat high mortality, especially among infants.

Smallpox was the first and most terrible epidemic to strike them. It came to the Indians of Eastern Canada in 1635 and spread right across the country scattering death as it went. The history of Russian Alaska hands down a record of the outbreak of 1837, which raged for four years, enveloped the whole coast and killed thousands of natives. In 1891, Father Barnum wrote of his visit to the ruins of three large caches which were filled with human bones. An aged native woman told him that she remembered the epidemic, and that those were the remains of the smallpox victims. Deaths had been so numerous that corpses had to be deposited in caches for lack of a better way of burial. Caches are small square structures on four high posts built for protection against dogs and other animals.

The second most deadly affliction was typhus. That came at the turn of the twentieth century. The third was pulmonary ailments such as tuberculosis. These diseases, if known at all before the advent of the white man, were very rare, so much so that the natives had developed no immunity to them.

In the days before civilization touched them, the natives suffered from ailments caused by malnutrition, but for these maladies they used specific remedies especially in the form of herbs. Premature senility among the tribes was induced by hardships. All studies of these primitive peoples indicate that malnutrition at that time was negligible compared to today.

While the epidemics have little chance of being controlled, the pulmonary diseases are not irresistible. The government with a limited budget has done what it could. In July, 1926, it provided a floating clinic with a doctor and two nurses for the Yukon River and its tributaries. The boat did excellent work for a number of years, yet it could hardly fringe the problem, for tuberculosis was known to be on a steady increase among the natives. From time to time Congress appropriates money for hospitals and further field nursing activities. A beginning has been made, but appropriations will have to be increased greatly if they are to meet the ever-mounting spread of tuberculosis.

Over and above the problem of the treatment of dis-

(Photo by Father Hubbard)

A newly born pup seal.

(Photo by Father Hubbard)

A food luxury for Eskimo—a white whale.

In a wilderness with practically no visitors, a Sunday evening boat
ride at the mission is a truly glorious thing.

Was it worth while?

ease, there is a great field of preventive work that has to do with food in Alaska and in our own country.

Perhaps the most momentous work in health and nutrition among the Eskimo has been done by Dr. Leuman M. Waugh, head of the School of Dental and Oral Surgery, Columbia University. His studies in Labrador and Alaska have shown conclusively that caries do not occur in primitives until the white man's food is taken to them. However, the startling part of his discovery is much more specific.

The foods traded to the natives by the white man when the native teeth first began to decay were refined flour, molasses, sugar and tea. The missionaries reported that wheat flour, both in bulk and as hard tack, had been used there before 1884 and that up to 1902 there had been no tooth complaints. It was when prospectors and traders supplied the natives with molasses and sugar that the teeth began to decay. The disease spread so fast that in two years the missionaries had to send for forceps for extraction of the teeth.

Dr. Waugh made a specific experiment on two groups: one group received a feeding of natural sugars (dates, figs, raisins, honey) each day; the second group received refined sugars (chewy candy, lollypops, etc.). In less than two months those fed on natural sugars had no new cavities, while in the group fed on refined sugars, a large proportion showed that decayed teeth had begun in that short experimental period.

In testing the mouths of twelve hundred Eskimo no caries were ever found among those who had not received refined sugar, candy or molasses. The sugar does not damage the teeth by way of the stomach but in a more direct manner. The sugar-yielding material—especially chewy candy which adheres to the teeth—feeds the particular bacteria present in the mouth, and the resultant acid eats through the enamel.

Notwithstanding the great inhospitality of that part of the world, with its nine or ten months of winter, the Eskimo were able to provide their bodies with all the mineral and vitamin requirements from seafoods, greens, berries, plants from the sea, and from eating the entire animal—flesh, blood, bone and contents of the stomach. A diet of straight seal-meat will keep a hunter in good health, but a diet that consists partly of tea and bread will sooner or later result in malnutrition.

Father LaFortune writes: "I am afraid the Eskimo will follow the Indians and disappear. It is hard to find the reason for it. Away from the whites except for two months every summer, the King Islanders are not spoiled. They don't drink; they live the same way their ancestors did, the only difference being that they now eat flour and sugar. When I came to Nome 30 years ago the men and women were stronger than the present generation. The next generation will be still weaker. In other places they disappear rapidly."

The gradual encroachment of the white man's diet is only part of the native's altered way of life. Other changes involve their hunting and fishing methods, their less healthful living conditions, and the clothing they wear. They are all part of one thing, the natives imitation of the white man, and the lack of foresight in the policy of exploitation which allows this to continue to its bitter end.

Before the white man came, the Eskimo considered it ridiculous to kill game for anything other than to feed and clothe himself and his family. For centuries their whole economy was in balance, the animals increased and decreased in cycles; there were always enough whales, walrus, seals. They used primitive methods of getting seal. For instance, one native would find a seal's breathing hole in the ice and after lying motionless for hours on his stomach awaiting the emergence of his prey, he would signal his partner to thrust the harpoon into the animal. Or, in the mild spring days when a seal came out to bask in the sunshine, the Eskimo would stalk him as he did land game. After approaching very near, he would throw his harpoon into the sleek body. Naturally it would require time and patience to get only one animal. Hunting methods were all personalized, and there was nothing in the way of mass production.

Then came the white man—the trappers and the traders. The natives gradually began to use steel tools, guns, ammunition, liquor. In payment they had to bring more and more furs. Now they are no longer killing to clothe and feed themselves. They are killing for skins, and they clothe and feed themselves through the trader. Their whole outlook has been changed. They are killing to get skins which they barter for food. With their traps they get as many fox as possible so that they can buy more and more of the shining cans of food they see on the shelves of the trader's store; and flour, tea, coffee and sugar as well. They are taking over the more useless of our kinds of food in place of the vitamin-filled food of their ancestors. The natives used to drink seal-blood broth in great quantity before they learned to drink tea and coffee. It was tasty, and it supplied the necessary strength and energy. Because they are doing the vigorous outdoor work which requires food energy, their new devitalized diet becomes increasingly bad for them as their bodies become more and more under-nourished. This is one reason why the tubercular death rate among the natives of Alaska is continually rising.

For centuries they had been a self-sufficient people: from the antler bone and ivory, they made harpoons, arrows, ice-chisels, needles, thimbles and other necessities. But the ivory tools gave way to weapons of iron; cooking vessels of clay, skin, bark and wood were replaced in the new order by metal pots; bows and arrows by firearms. Once a tribe had made these changes it could not go back to its former conditions because it had lost most of its earlier skills such as chipping knives and arrowheads of flint, grinding out stone axes and fashioning serviceable bows. The natives were now entirely dependent on the trading posts.

This industrial revolution in their lives strongly affected their general living conditions.

Eskimo from the Bering Strait southward used a pottery lamp burning oil from the blubber of the sea mammals, while in other sections of the country they used the same sort of lamp fashioned of stone. The blubber lamp was their own creation: it gave them the right amount of heat; it suited their kind of life, and it always maintained a low temperature in the house. Even if there was a pile of food in the corner, the low temperature would prevent it from becoming rancid, or fermenting. Today, the Eskimo buy the primus (or coal oil) stove which gives much more heat and brings the temperature up to from 45 to 60 degrees. Needless to say, the food which is kept in the corner becomes too warm and produces a bad odor as well as decidedly unhealthy conditions.

Their summer housing has also been influenced by the white man's ways. The conical type opening at the top in the original Indian tent provided perfect ventilation. But the kind of tent which the natives have been adopting from civilization retains too much heat and produces a bad draft. Again, any surplus of food becomes corrupted because of the greater heat.

The adoption of the white man's garb in these severely cold regions has also been unfortunate. It is said that the Eskimo's complete clothing, weighing only about five pounds, is warmer and more satisfactory than woolen garments twice the weight. Misguided imitation of the white man prompts many Eskimo now to wear woolen underclothes, and even complete costumes from civilization, despite the fact that their loose-fitting garments made of caribou fur are watertight, more picturesque, more hygienic, and offer greater protection against the intense cold.

Those who have taken over the white man's dress

often wear one pair of pants over another, both of
which soon become filthy and worn out. In the old days
a good hunter would have a new parka and not wear
the worn-out one: or if he could not have a new one,
his wife would meticulously sew round patches on the
old garment and so make it entirely watertight.

The natives had a good way of life, and it ought to
be preserved. Some strong statements have been made
about the dire need of social reconstruction and scientific aid. Perhaps it has been stated most directly by
Dr. Victor E. Levine of Creighton University, who during seven trips to Alaska has made medical and bio-
logical surveys among the Eskimo, once working for
the winter with Father Hubbard's party on King Island.
He and Professor Bauer, as a result of their work, made
this startling statement. "Due to susceptibility to tuberculosis and other diseases, the average life span of the
Eskimo of Alaska is only twenty years, and their race
is doomed to extinction within a few generations unless
modern medical science comes to their aid."

XXI
The Oldest Bishop Carries On

IN JUNE of 1941 Bishop Crimont in Juneau told me of his arrival forty-seven years earlier at Dutch Harbor. It was here that he first exercised the sacred ministry in Alaskan territory: he buried an Eskimo chief who had been his shipmate. Just one year later in New York the radio told me of the Japanese planes arriving at Dutch Harbor.

THE ICE HAD gone down the river one spring day in 1901, the snow had disappeared from the ground, and a few violets were already pushing their way through it. The boys at Holy Cross were urging their Superior to accompany them on a picnic a few miles away, but he could not spare the time. By afternoon, however, he decided to join them after all, and walked fast and steadily to their chosen spot. The exertion made him perspire freely so that a few hours later when the chill air of the early evening overtook him, the sudden change had devastating effects. Joseph Crimont came down with inflammatory rheumatism which became so acute that it forced him to bed for a month.

By the middle of the summer he was still pale and wan, though on his feet again, when the Very Reverend Father de la Motte made an official visitation of the missions. Father Crimont looked badly enough to be given attention, the visitor decided, and sent the young missionary to Gonzaga College at Spokane.

So it was that the ordinary hardships—the hazardous trips over the tundra, the gnat and mosquito-ridden summers—had nothing to do with his temporary leave. A mild and seemingly harmless activity was the cause. After a week's rest he was made Rector of the College.

A number of Jesuits in Spokane at that time long remembered the missionary-made Rector. The late Father

Meagher, famous for his world-wide missionary activities, used to seek advice from Father Crimont who, he said, would always look at the crucifix before giving an answer. Others said his retreat sermons and instructions were inspired and penetrating and that they had never forgotten them. This work continued but three years, for Alaska called again.

In 1904, Father Crimont was appointed successor to Very Reverend John B. Rene, S.J., Prefect Apostolic of Alaska, and he immediately began his visits over the territory. At Eagle he met Father Monroe and took him to the Tanana Valley to survey the possibilities for a mission. The future town of Fairbanks consisted of only a half-dozen frame houses and a few canvas tents. With the aid of a little crowd, an organist and singers, the first public mass was said on July 3rd in the court building. On July 4th a grand patriotic parade swept over the newly levelled streets from which the trees had just been felled. A few days later the two missionaries rowed their small boat down the Chena, the Tanana and the Yukon Rivers while gnats and mosquitoes attacked perspiring arms and faces, and while sand bars and eddies made the long trip a hazardous one.

Thus ten years after his arrival in the territory, Father Crimont had been appointed head of the missions there. From this time on as administrator, he was destined to spend his life living more out of a suitcase than in a residence. His summers were passed in visiting his far-flung missions, administering confirmation and untangling the problems at hand. Until 1912 the winters found him with Father Monroe in Fairbanks. This young growing town was a small part of the work of these two priests. In addition they visited on foot hundreds of miles of surrounding mining country. The old miners and prospectors still talk of seeing them many times in icy water up to their hips dragging logs up to the site for the building of a chapel or house.

Meanwhile Alaska was growing: the rich gold deposits were attracting thousands of men, salmon canneries were thriving, hundreds of fishing boats were finding profitable new waters, trappers and traders were increasing, and the homestead law was encouraging settlers to take up unsurveyed land without cost.

The Catholic Church grew apace providing churches, hospitals, boarding and day schools for natives and whites, resident missionaries in the native hunting and fishing villages. Through all this development the Prefect Apostolic was at the helm, guiding in his quiet, sure way the policies of the church, and being a profound influence throughout the territory. "He was a man with a gentle soul and a great spirit whom you felt better for knowing."

Then came the year of 1917 when Pope Benedict XV conferred a bishopric on the Most Reverend Joseph Raphael Crimont. When the news came to him, he wrote to his Superior:

"If it is God's will to glorify Himself in me by choosing this helpless pauper and raising him from the dust and placing him among the princes of the church, let it be so. I did not ask for it, nor expect it . . . I am not scared, and do not refuse it. I don't intend to resign from it."

He placed on his coat of arms "la rose effeuillée," for he had long been especially devoted to his compatriot, Terese of Lisieux.

The essential simplicity which remained with him through the years shows itself in incidents along the way. In Seattle after his consecration he went to buy a gold-plated Bishop's candlestick. When the clerk asked where he should send it, Bishop Crimont said he would take it along, which he did by unscrewing the two parts and stuffing one into each side pocket.

Victor Hugo in describing his Bishop in *Les Misérables*, wrote: "Who can be in contact continually with all the distresses, all misfortunes, all privations without taking upon himself a little of that holy poverty, like the dust of a journey?"

But Bishop Crimont's poverty was not like this: it was ever a part of him, like the blue of his eyes and the warmth of his heart. He wore it like a suit that fitted him without alteration. He carried it out in his clothes, his food, his Episcopal residence, which always remained the same, a small two-story frame house which usually needed painting.

Ever since his consecration he has bought nothing for his priestly wardrobe. His cassocks were made over from those sent by the Extension Society. Since Monsignori purple was near enough to be usable for a Bishop, a Monsignor in the Middle West used to send him clothes which he gladly accepted. December sometimes found him wearing a light top coat while on a trip in the States. He protested that his winters in Alaska had inured him to the cold, but his friends understood him despite, not because of his words, and insisted on buying him a heavy coat. Though he could not bear to spend money on himself, yet he did not let its scarcity affect him. He went ahead establishing new missions without money and expecting them to go on. Somehow they did go on.

He was incorrigible in giving things away. Once a beautiful rug was given him expressly for his own use. But he sent it to a missionary who he said needed it more than he. His friends sent him money to use on himself, but they knew that his habits were stronger than their influence.

Since 1912 when part of each year was spent in Juneau, he has administered the diocese of five thousand nine hundred square miles from his little office on the second floor of St. Ann's Rectory there. During this time he has not had a secretary but has written all his letters, either personal or business, in his own exquisite handwriting. Literally thousands of them are cherished as precious possessions throughout the country. He brings to each letter an unusual gift of expression, a kind of personalized beauty of phrase and depth of feeling. One of his fellow Bishops said that Bishop Crimont had the sweetest pen he had ever known.

He surpasses others in the generosity of his friendship. He likes people, and has such a profound effect on those he meets, that they go away, as one has said, "with a desire to be worthy of such a trust." When the Bishop becomes anyone's friend, he goes on always being a friend, even though the person later proves himself unworthy. When asked to explain this, he answered simply: "Ah, but God goes on loving people, doesn't He? He is slow in changing and why are not we? God loves His saints, but He loves a sinner too." Like Father Bede Jarrett, he would rather occasionally be taken advantage of than live in permanent suspicion of others.

While attending an annual meeting of Bishops twenty years ago, he had an afternoon with a group of new friends. Showing them the map of Alaska, he pointed out the missions which needed special help. As a result of these few hours, the ladies formed a League and worked up a rummage sale that first summer which netted one thousand dollars. Each year for fifteen years after, they sent money for his missions.

During his winters in Juneau his time was shared between his duties as Bishop and those as parish priest. When he was nearly seventy years old there was still no bridge across the Bay from Juneau to Douglas. But the Bishop would never let a younger man do the harder tasks for him. He could be seen walking down the winter's icy streets to the dock, there to take a boat to Douglas where he would say Mass.

In 1925 Bishop Crimont and Bishop Schuler, S.J., of El Paso led the American pilgrimage to Rome, and Lisieux. This was Bishop Crimont's first trip to Europe since the early nineties, and he was accompanied by

Rev. G. Edgar Gallant, the first priest ordained in Alaska. At the end of September the pilgrims returned to Lisieux from Rome, and the Bishop said Mass in the Infirmary where St. Terese had died twenty-eight years before. At the Mass the Little Flower's three sisters received communion from the hand of their newly adopted brother. Earlier in the summer the Bishop first met Mother Agnes (Martin) when they began a lasting friendship.

While he was in Rome the Sacred Congregation decreed St. Terese the Queen and Patroness of Alaska, a title the Bishop had offered her five years earlier. From this time on his devotion to the Little Flower became one of the great influences of his life. Beginning with the reading of "Histoire d'un Ame," many things contributed to feed the devotion: blessings obtained by himself, miracles told by others, important favors received by Father Ruppert. After the visit to Lisieux the Bishop distributed many relics of the Little Flower and did much to spread devotion to her. Application of a relic to a Sister Superior of Douglas brought immediate cure of a serious illness. An insane woman in Juneau when shown a picture of the Little Flower, fell asleep the first time in over a week. Her cure was also immediate and permanent.

Through these years the Bishop's health was generally good. In November 1932 he had his remaining teeth extracted, and wrote: "they came out as if enchanted by the dentist's instruments." In the spring of 1934 when landing at Marshall on the Yukon River, he stumbled as he walked up the gangplank, whirled around and fell on a rock. He broke a few ribs and could not continue his trip. Two years later while visiting the missions he was bitten by big black lice. The larvae multiplied rapidly, lodging themselves beneath the outer layer of the skin while producing an itching which allowed of neither sleep nor rest. The malady caused him to spend two months in St. Joseph' Hospital in Fairbanks. "At the end of the long process," he wrote, "in compensation of their depredations, they made me a present of a new tailored suit of skin, fitting me like a glove."

In 1937 the Bishop and Father Coudeyre had a long audience with Pope Pius XI who called Alaska "the hardest mission."

"The guide I had on my excursions to the Alps," he said, speaking in French, "was the same who had served as a guide to the Duke of Abruzzi when the latter explored Alaska. I am very much interested in Alaska and its missions."

When they spoke of ages and His Holiness and the Bishop were found to be practically the same age, Pope Pius said to the Bishop: "Les glaces vous preservent."

In October 1939 while attending a banquet in honor of the consecration of Bishop Condon of Great Falls, Bishop Crimont walked too close to the edge of the elevated table and slipped down off the platform. He took the night train to Portland and the next morning could not move from his berth. Four ribs had been broken. In December of that year a Coadjutor, Walter

J. Fitzgerald, S.J. was appointed to take over some of the excessive work of the vicariate.

A half year after this, Bishop Crimont had occasion to call on the Little Flower in a very special way. While recuperating from an icy fall on Palm Sunday, His Excellency was given as a tonic Blaud's Pills. One of them caused him violent distress, and the next morning an X-ray showed the pill to be lodged in the left bronchus, in a position too difficult for extraction. A trip to Seattle for an operation seemed the only solution, but there were grave doubts as to its outcome after the lapse of so much time.

Then it was that Sister Mary Gabriella placed a relic of St. Terese just over the position of the pill. The Bishop rested quietly until the middle of the next day when a violent spasm of coughing brought the pill, still undissolved, into his mouth. It had been lodged in the bronchus for forty hours. The doctors were surprised, and no one had any doubt who was responsible for the cure.

The following year the Bishop wrote: "I have an incurable disease, old age, to which each day adds its quota," but he kept going about his work as though he were thirty years younger. At the end of that summer he made a trip to Bellingham, Washington, to give the address at the Profession of the Sisters of St. Joseph of Newark.

On July 29, 1942, Most Rev. Joseph Raphael Crimont, S.J., the oldest Bishop of America, celebrated his Silver Episcopal Jubilee in the Cathedral at Seattle where he had been consecrated. Of his 84 years, 45 had been spent in Alaska, 25 as its first Bishop.

The Bishop saw God in everybody. This abiding sense showed in all his actions, for the people he talked with felt their own dignity, a holy confidence in themselves, and a feeling of their own potential goodness. They got it not from anything he said or left unsaid, but from his manner. The force of his belief shone from his eyes and directed his actions. He focused his holiness and zeal on everyone he met and lifted them up.

If we seek the records of his achievements we shall find them not in monuments of stone, for he built no Cathedrals; not in a materially prosperous diocese—his is still a poor one—but in the extraordinary influence he exercised upon those whose lives moved in the shadow of his own.

St. Terese of Lisieux speaking to her Sisters of what she would do when asked to pray for favors when she would be in Heaven, said: "First I shall take care to look into the Face of God, to ascertain if it is His Will to grant the favor, then I shall act accordingly."

This is the great secret and lesson for us to master when we wish for favors: See to it that our will and the Will of God are one. Ask not only for our own sakes, but at the same time for the sake of God, the Giver of all gifts, Who is not only a loving Father, a loving Friend to us, but also an Educator seeing to our greatest and ultimate good.

+ Joseph R. Crimont, S.J.
Vic. Ap. of Alaska

Index

I. Geographical Names

230 INDEX

II. Persons